WITHDRAWN

For Reference

Not to be taken from this room

Seal of the State of Vermont

CHRONOLOGY AND DOCUMENTARY HANDBOOK OF THE STATE OF
VERMONT

ROBERT I. VEXLER

State Editor

WILLIAM F. SWINDLER

Series Editor

1979 OCEANA PUBLICATIONS, INC./ Dobbs Ferry, New York

Ref
F
49.5
.C45

Library of Congress Cataloging in Publication Data

Main entry under title:

Chronology and documentary handbook of the State of Vermont.

(Chronologies and documentary handbooks of the States; 45)
Bibliography: p.
Includes index.
SUMMARY: A history of Vermont in chronological format, with supporting documents, biographical outlines of chief State politicians and prominent personalities, and a name index.
    1. Vermont—History—Chronology.   2. Vermont—Biography.   3. Vermont—History—Sources.
[1. Vermont—History]   I. Vexler, Robert I.
II. Series.
F49.5.C45   974.3'002'02   78-26322
ISBN 0-379-16170-2

© Copyright 1979 by Oceana Publications, Inc.

All rights reserved. No part of this publication may be reproduced or transmitted in any form or by any means, electronic or mechanical, including photocopy, recording, xerography, or any information storage and retrieval system, without permission in writing from the publisher.

Manufactured in the United State of America

TABLE OF CONTENTS

INTRODUCTION ix

CHRONOLOGY (1608-1977) 1

BIOGRAPHICAL DIRECTORY 19

PROMINENT PERSONALITIES 41

FIRST STATE CONSTITUTIONS 47

SELECTED DOCUMENTS 75
    Vermont in 1791 77
    Legends of Springfield 87
    Vermont - 1893 109
    Vermont - 1920's 127
    Basic Facts 143
    Map of Congressional Districts 144

SELECTED BIBLIOGRAPHY 145

NAME INDEX 147

ACKNOWLEDGMENT

Special recognition should be accorded Melvin Hecker, whose research has made a valuable contribution to this volume.

Thanks to my wife, Francine, in appreciation of her help in the preparation of this work.

Thanks also to my children, David and Melissa, without whose patience and understanding I would have been unable to devote the considerable time necessary for completing the state chronology series.

I also wish to acknowledge the scholarly research grant given to me by Pace University. This greatly eased the technical preparation of this work.

Robert I. Vexler
Pace University

INTRODUCTION

This projected series of *Chronologies and Documentary Handbooks of the States* will ultimately comprise fifty separate volumes—one for each of the states of the Union. Each volume is intended to provide a concise ready reference to basic data on the state, and to serve as a starting point for more extended study as the individual user may require. Hopefully, it will be a guidebook for a better informed citizenry - students, civic and service organizations, professional and business personnel, and others.

The editorial plan for the *Handbook* series falls into six divisions: (1) a chronology of selected events in the history of the state; (2) a short biographical directory of the principal public officials, e.g., governors, Senators and Representatives; (3) a short biographical directory of prominent personalities of the state (for most states); (4) the first state constitution; (5) the text of some representative documents illustrating main currents in the political, economic, social or cultural history of the state; and (6) a selected bibliography for those seeking further or more detailed information. Most of the data found in the present volume, in fact, have been taken from one or another of these references.

The current constitutions of all fifty states, as well as the federal Constitution, are regularly kept up to date in the definitive collection maintained by the Legislative Drafting Research of Columbia University and published by the publisher of the present series of *Handbooks*. These texts are available in most major libraries under the title, *Constitutions of the United States: National and State,* in two volumes, with a companion volume, the *Index Digest of State Constitutions.*

Finally, the complete collection of documents illustrative of the constitutional development of each state, from colonial or territorial status up to the current constitution as found in the Columbia University collection, is being prepared for publication in a multi-volume series by the present series editor. Whereas the present series of *Handbooks* is intended for a wide range of interested citizens, the series of annotated constitutional materials in the volumes of *Sources and Documents of U.S. Constitutions* is primarily for the specialist in government, history or law. This is not to suggest that the general citizenry may not profit equally from referring to these materials; rather it points up the separate purpose of the *Handbooks*, which is to guide the user of these and other sources of authoritative information with which he may systematically enrich his knowledge of this state and its place in the American Union.

William J. Swindler
John Marshall Professor of Law
College of William and Mary
Series Editor

Robert I. Vexler
Associate Professor of History
Pace University
Series Associate Editor

Freedom and Unity
State Motto

CHRONOLOGY

1608	Samuel de Champlain, the governor of Quebec, travelled down the St. Lawrence River to Lake Champlain.
1609	July. Samuel de Champlain entered the present state of Vermont in an expedition against the Iroquois Indian tribe. He thus laid a basis for a French claim to the territory.
1666	The French constructed their first settlement in Vermont, Fort Sainte Anne on the Isle de la Motte in Lake Champlain. It was located near the present-day border between the state of Vermont and Canada.
1668	Bishop de Laval of Quebec went to Fort Sainte Anne on the Isle de la Motte where he conducted services for the troops.
1690	Captain Jacobus de Warm of Great Britain led an expedition from Albany against the French. He and his troops constructed a trading post at Chimney Point in Addison Township.
1704	The French attacked Deerfield.
1724	Massachusetts residents established the first permanent white settlement at Fort Dummer, near present-day Dummer in the southeastern part of the town of Brattleboro.
1731	The French constructed Fort Frederic at the narrowest point of Lake Champlain.
1741	King George II of England assigned the territory including the following settlements to New Hampshire: Sartwell's Fort and Bridgman's Fort in the township of Vernon and Fort Hill in the township of Putney. The region had been in dispute between Massachusetts and New Hampshire.
1761-63	New Hampshire Governor John Wentworth issued 108 grants. Settlements were organized in Brattleboro, Putney, Westminster, Halifax, Marlborough, Wilmington, New Fare, Rockingham, Townsend, and Dummerston. All of these were located in Windham County. Vernon (or Hinsdale) was also established in

Cheshire County.

1764   July 20. The privy council issued a proclamation recognizing the New York claims. The settlers in Vermont were soon ordered to surrender their patents and purchase the land again from the authorities in Albany. Seth Warner and Remember Baker, following the lead of Ethan Allen, refused to do so.

1770   Estimated population: 10,000

1771   Colonel Ethan Allen formed a regular military force among the inhabitants living in the area west of the mountains which became known as the Green Mountain Boys.

1775   March 13. The residents of Cumberland County rioted at Westminster against the royal authorities. Two people were killed.

May 10. Ethan Allen and his Green Mountain Boys, aided by some people from Connecticut and Benedict Arnold, captured Fort Ticonderoga and then went into Canada under the leadership of Montgomery and Schuyler.

1776   October 11. British and American ships (the last under the command of Benedict Arnold) fought on Lake Champlain. Arnold and his ships escaped and arrived at Crown Point on October 14.

1777   January 15. The Vermont residents declared their independence as a republic called New Connecticut.

June. General John Burgoyne and his army stopped at Crown Point on their way to Fort Ticonderoga.

July 2-8. Vermont drafted its constitution. It became the first state to abolish slavery and to adopt universal male suffrage with no property qualifications.

July 7. The Battle of Hubbardtown was fought.

August. American troops led by John Stark defeated the British and Hessians at the Battle of Bennington.

CHRONOLOGY 3

1778	Thomas Chittenden became governor of Vermont. He served in the office until 1789.
1779	February. Vermont rejected the sixteen New Hampshire towns which wished to join with it.

February 11. Bennington County, with Bennington and Manchester as its seats, was created. It was named for Benning Wentworth, provincial governor of New Hampshire who gave 500 acres to Dartmouth College. |
| 1780 | Estimated population: 47,620.

The first paper in Vermont was published briefly at Westminster, the *Vermont Gazette*.

The British raided Royalton from Canada, but they did not remain long. |
| 1781 | February 22. Orange, Rutland, Windham and Windsor Counties were created. Orange, with Chelsea as its seat, was named for Prince William IV of Orange.

Rutland, with its seat at Rutland City, was named for Rutland, Massachusetts, which in turn had been named for Rutland, England.

Windham, with New Fare as its seat, was named for Windham, Connecticut. Windsor, with its seat at Woodstock, was named for Windsor, England.

New Hampshire's valley towns along with some New York towns to the west were admitted to Vermont. General George Washington intervened in the dispute, suggesting that if Vermont returned the towns, Congress would admit it as the 14th state. Vermont complied in 1782, but Congress did not admit the state. |
| 1782 | Difficulties with New Hampshire were settled. The west bank of the Connecticut River was accepted as the final boundary. New York refused to give up its claims until 1790. |

VERMONT

1785	October 18. Addison County, with Middlebury as its seat, was established. It was named for Joseph Addison, English under secretary of state, Member of Parliament and editor of the <u>Spectator</u>.
1786	Vermont adopted its constitution.
	200 farmers met in Rutland, indicating their displeasure with actions of lawyers who were forcing many people into prisons for debt.
	Vermont adopted a law which prohibited the sale of Blacks or their removal from its borders.
1787	October 22. Chittenden County, with its seat at Burlington, was created. It was named for Thomas Chittenden, first governor of the colonial assembly, first president of the Committee of Safety, and territorial governor of Vermont.
1789	Moses Robinson became governor of Vermont. He served in the office until 1790.
1790	Population: 85,425.
	October 28. New York relinquished its claims to Vermont in return for a payment of $30,000 by Vermont.
	Thomas Chittenden, Federalist, became governor of Vermont. He continued to serve in the office after Vermont became a state until his death on August 25, 1797.
1791	March 4. Vermont was admitted to the Union as the 14th state.
	November 3. The state legislature ratified the first Ten Amendments to the United States Constitution, the Bill of Rights.
	The University of Vermont received its charter in Burlington. Its first degrees were granted in 1804.
1792	November 5. Caledonia, Essex, Franklin and Orleans Counties were created. Caledonia, with its seat at St. Johnsburg, was named for the old name for Scotland.

Essex, with Guildhall as its seat, was named for Essex County, England and Robert Devereux, Earl of Essex.

Franklin, with its seat at St. Albans, was named for Benjamin Franklin, American official, member of the Continental Congress, signer of the Declaration of Independence and delegate to the Constitutional Convention.

Orleans County has its seat at Newport City.

Colonel Ewel Hale completed construction of the first important wooden truss bridge, adapted to American needs, at Bellows Falls.

1793	A new state constitution was adopted.
1794	October 9 - November 9. The state legislature ratified the 11th Amendment to the United States Constitution.

Vermont's oldest paper, The Rutland Herald, was first published as a weekly. It is now a daily paper.

1797   August 25. Lieutenant Governor Paul Brigham, Federalist, became acting governor of the state upon the death of Governor Thomas Chittenden. Brigham served in the post until October 16, 1797.

October 16. Isaac Tichenor, Federalist, became governor of Vermont. He served in the office until 1807.

1800   Population: 154,465.

November 1. Middlebury College received its charter in Middlebury. It granted the first degrees in 1802.

November 9. Grand Isle County, with its seat at North Hero, was created. It was organized November 2, 1805, effective December 1, 1805.

1804   January 30. The state legislature ratified the 12th Amendment to the United States Constitution.

1807	Israel Smith, Democrat-Republican, became governor of the state. He served in the office until 1808.
1808	The capital of the state was permanently located at Montpelier.
	The first lake-going steamship in the world set sail from Burlington on Lake Champlain.
	Isaac Tichenor, Federalist, again became governor of Vermont. He served in the post until 1809.
1809	Jonas Galusha, Democrat-Republican, became governor of the state. He remained in the office until 1813.
1810	Population: 217,895.
	November 1. Washington County, with Montpelier as its seat, was created. It was organized October 16, 1811, effective December 1, 1811. It was named for George Washington, commander of all the Continental Armies during the Revolutionary War and first President of the United States.
1813	Martin Chittenden, Federalist, became governor of the state. He served in the post until 1815.
	Fort Cassin in the northwest corner of present-day Addison County, was defended against the British. This was part of the activity during the War of 1812.
1815	Jonas Galusha, Democrat-Republican, became governor of Vermont. He served in the office until 1820.
1819	Norwich University was founded at Northfield. This institution made a significant contribution to American higher education because of its emphasis on technical training which was only carried out at the United States Military Academy at West Point.
1820	Population: 235,981.
	Richard Skinner, Democrat-Republican, became governor of the state. He remained in the

CHRONOLOGY

office until 1823.

1823   With the opening of the Champlain Canal, trade was carried between Troy, Albany, and New York City, rather than to Canada.

Cornelius P. Van Ness, Democrat-Republican, became governor of the state. He served in the post until 1826.

Lewis Danning hired Stephen Abbot, a coach builder. The two men soon became partners and began building the Concord Coach.

1826   Ezra Butler, Democrat-Republican, became governor of the state. He served in the office until 1828.

1828   William Lloyd Garrison began editing the *Journal of the Times*.

Samuel C. Crafts, National Republican, became governor of Vermont, remaining in the office until 1831.

1830   Population: 280,652.

October 5. Chester A. Arthur, 21st President of the United States, was born in Fairfield.

1831   William A. Palmer, Anti-Masonic Fusionist, became governor of the state. He served until 1835.

1834   Thomas Davenport, a blacksmith, built an electric motor which had the basic design of the standard electric motor of today.

1835   October 26. Lamoille County, with its seat at Hyde Park, was created. It was a corruption of La Mouette, the name which Champlain gave to the river.

Silas H. Jennison, Whig, became acting governor of Vermont and continued to serve until 1836 because no governor was elected by the voters. Jennison was subsequently elected and served as governor until 1841.

1839   John Humphrey Noyes established his experimental community at Putney. The community broke up in 1847.

VERMONT

1841	Charles Paine, Whig, became governor of Vermont. He served in the office until 1843.
1843	The Chambly Canal was opened, thus bypassing the Richelieu Rapids to Montreal and Quebec.
	John Matlocks, Whig, became governor of the state, remaining in the office until 1844.
1844	William Slade, Whig, became governor of Vermont. He served in the post until 1848.
1848	The first railroad was opened in the state.
	Carlos Coolidge, Whig, became governor of the state in which post he remained until 1850.
1849	March 8. Jacob Collamer became Postmaster General of the United States in the Administration of President Zachary Taylor.
1850	Population: 314,120.
	Carter K. Williams, Whig, became governor of Vermont. He served in the gubernatorial office until 1852.
1852	Erastus Fairbanks, Whig, became governor of the state. He served until 1853.
1853	John S. Robinson, Whig, became governor of Vermont, remaining in the office until 1854.
1854	July 13. The Republican Party was organized in the state.
	Stephen Royce, Whig and Republican, became governor. He served in the post until 1856.
1856	Ryland Fletcher, Republican, became governor of Vermont, remaining in the office until 1858.
1858	Hiland Hall, Republican, became governor of the state. He served until 1860.
1860	Population: 315,098.

CHRONOLOGY 9

Erastus Fairbanks, Republican, again became governor of Vermont. He served in the office until 1861.

1861 Frederick Holbrook, Republican, became governor of the state. He served in the post until 1863.

1862 Vermont's Senator Justin Morrill developed and was instrumental in the passage of the Land Grant College Act.

1863 John Gregory Smith, Republican, became governor of Vermont in which post he remained until 1865.

1864 May 19. Nathaniel Hawthorne died in Plymouth.

October 19. Lieutenant B. H. Young and a small group of Confederate troops crossed the Canadian border and raided the town of St. Albans. One resident was killed, several wounded, and $200,000 taken from the vaults of the local banks.

1865 March 9. The state legislature ratified the 13th Amendment to the United States Constitution.

Paul Dillingham, Republican, became governor of the state. He served in the office until 1867.

The State Agricultural College was established at Burlington.

1867 John B. Page, Republican, became governor of Vermont, remaining in the post until 1869.

Castleton State College was established at Castleton. It opened in 1868.

1869 October 20. The state legislature ratified the 15th Amendment to the United States Constitution.

Peter T. Washburn, Republican, became governor of the state. He served in the office until his death on February 7, 1870.

VERMONT

1870   Population: 330,551.

February 7. Lieutenant Governor George W. Hendee, Republican, became governor of Vermont upon the death of Governor Peter T. Washburn. Hendee served in the post until the end of the term in 1870.

St. Albans was the site of an attempted Fenian invasion of Canada.

John W. Stewart, Republican, became governor of the state and served in the office until 1872.

1872   July 4. Calvin Coolidge, who was later to be the 30th President of the United States, was born at Plymouth Notch.

Julius Convers, Republican, became governor of Vermont, remaining in the post until 1874.

1874   Asahel Peck, Republican, became governor and served in the office until 1876.

1876   Horace Fairbanks, Republican, became governor of Vermont in which post he remained until 1878.

1878   Redfield Proctor, Republican, became governor of the state. He served in the office until 1880.

1880   Population: 332,286.

Roswell Farnham, Republican, became governor of Vermont. He served in the post until 1882.

1881   Chester A. Arthur, who had been born in Fairfield, became the 21st President of the United States upon the assassination of President James Abram Garfield.

1882   Joel L. Barstow, Republican, became governor of Vermont, remaining in the office until 1884.

CHRONOLOGY

1884	Samuel E. Pingree, Republican, became governor of the state, serving in the office until 1886.
1886	Ebenezer J. Ormsbee, Republican, became governor of Vermont, serving in the post until 1888.
1888	William P. Dillingham, Republican, became governor of the state. He served in the office until 1890.
1889	March 5. Redfield Proctor became United States Secretary of War in the Cabinet of President Benjamin Harrison.
1890	Population: 332,422
	Carroll S. Page, Republican, became governor of the state and remained in the office until 1892.
1892	Levi K. Fuller, Republican, became governor of the state. He served in the office until 1894.
1894	Urban A. Woodbury, Republican, became governor of the state. He remained in the post until 1896.
1896	Josiah Grout, Republican, became governor of Vermont, serving in the office until October 6, 1898.
1898	October 6. Edward C. Smith, Republican, became governor of Vermont. He served in the office until October 4, 1900.
1900	Population: 343,641.
	October 4. William W. Stickney, Republican, became governor of the state. He served in the office until October 3, 1902.
1902	October 3. John G. McCullough, Republican, became governor of the state. He served in the post until October 6, 1904.
1904	October 6. Charles J. Bell, Republican, became governor of the state. He served in the office until October 4, 1906.
	St. Michael's College was founded at Winooski.

1906	October 4. Fletcher D. Proctor, Republican, became governor of Vermont, serving in the post until October 8, 1908.
1908	October 8. George H. Prouty, Republican, became governor of the state. He remained in the office until October 5, 1910.
1910	Population: 355,956.
	October 5. John A. Mead, Republican, became governor of Vermont. He served in the office until October 3, 1912.
1912	October 3. Allen M. Fletcher, Republican, became governor of the state. He served in the post until January 7, 1915, the date for inauguration of the governor having been changed.
1913	February 19. The state legislature ratified the 16th Amendment to the United States Constitution.
	February 24. The state legislature ratified the 17th Amendment to the United States Constitution.
1915	January 7. Charles W. Gates, Republican, who had been elected in 1915, became governor of Vermont. He served until January 4, 1917.
1917	January 4. Horace F. Graham, Republican, who had been elected in 1916, became governor of the state. He served in the office until January 9, 1919.
1919	January 9. Percival W. Clement, Republican, who had been elected in 1918, became governor of the state. He served in the post until January 6, 1921.
	January 29. The state legislature ratified the 18th Amendment to the United States Constitution.
1920	Population: 352,428.
1921	January 6. James Hartness, Republican, who had been elected in 1920, became governor of Vermont. He served in the office until January 4, 1923.

February 8. The state legislature ratified the 19th Amendment to the United States Constitution.

March 5. Albert B. Fall became United States Secretary of the Interior in the Cabinet of President Warren G. Harding.

1923   January 4. Redfield Proctor, Republican, who had been elected in 1922, became governor of the state. He served in the office until January 8, 1925.

August 2. Calvin Coolidge, who had been born in Plymouth Notch, became 30th President of the United States upon the death of President Warren G. Harding.

1925   January 8. Franklin S. Billings, Republican, who had been elected in 1924, became governor of the state. He served in the post until January 6, 1922.

March 17. John G. Sargent was appointed United States Attorney General by President Calvin Coolidge. Sargent assumed his office as a member of the cabinet on March 18.

Trinity College was founded in Burlington.

1927   January 6. John E. Weeks, Republican, who had been elected in 1926, became governor of the state. He was reelected in 1928 and served in the office until January 8, 1931.

One of the worst floods in Vermont's history occurred, killing 60 persons and causing millions of dollars in damage.

1930   Population: 359,611.

The first radio station in the state, WSYS, began broadcasting at Rutland.

1931   January 8. Stanley C. Wilson, Republican, who had been elected in 1930, became governor of the state. He was reelected in 1932 and served until January 10, 1935.

1932   Fall. Bennington College for women opened. This institution was an experiment in progressive education which did not use the orthodox methods of grading and credits.

VERMONT

1933 — February 2. The state legislature ratified the 20th Amendment to the United States Constitution.

September 23. The state legislature ratified the 21st Amendment to the United States Constitution.

1935 — January 10. Charles M. Smith, Republican, who had been elected in 1934, became governor of the state. He remained in the office until January 7, 1937.

1937 — January 7. George D. Aiken, Republican, who had been elected in 1936, became governor of the state. He was reelected in 1938 and served in the post until January 9, 1941.

1938 — Goddard College was founded in Plainfield.

1940 — Population: 358,231.

1941 — January 9. William Henry Wills, Republican, who had been elected in 1940, became governor of the state. He served in the office until January 1945, having been reelected 19 1942.

1944 — Lyndon State College was established in Lyndonville.

1945 — January. Mortimer Robinson Proctor, Republican, who had been elected in 1944, became governor of the state. He served in the post until January 9, 1947.

1947 — January 9. Ernest W. Gibson, Republican, who had been elected in 1946, became governor of the state. He served in the office until his resignation on January 16, 1950, having been reelected in 1948.

April 15. The state legislature ratified the 22nd Amendment to the United States Constitution.

Marlboro College was founded at Marlboro.

1950 — Population: 377,747.

January 16. Lieutenant Governor Harold J. Arthur, Republican, became governor of the

state upon the resignation of Governor Ernest
W. Gibson. Arthur served in the office until the end of the term on January 4, 1951.

1951 January 4. Lee W. Emerson, Republican, who
had been elected in 1950, became governor
of Vermont. He was reelected in 1952 and
served in the post until January 6, 1955.

1954 The first television station in the state,
WCAX-TV, began broadcasting from Burlington.

The College of St. Joseph the Provider was
established at Rutland.

1955 January 6. Joseph R. Robinson, Republican,
who had been elected in 1954, became governor
of the state, He was reelected in 1956 and
served in the post until January 8, 1959.

1959 January 8. Robert T. Stafford, Republican,
who had been elected in 1958, became governor
of Vermont. He served in the office until
January 5, 1961.

1960 Population: 389,881.

Windham College was founded at Putney.

1961 January 5. Frank Ray Keyser, Jr., Republican, who had been elected in 1960, became
governor of Vermont. He served in the office
until January 10, 1963.

1963 January 10. Philip H. Hoff, was in 1962
was elected the first Democratic governor
in the state since 1853, took office. He
was reelected in 1964 and 1966, serving
until January 9, 1969.

March 15. The state legislature ratified
the 24th Amendment to the United States
Constitution.

1964 Vermont residents voted for Lyndon B. Johnson as the first Democrat ever to receive
a majority in a presidential election in the
state.

1965 The state legislature voted to restrict the
death penalty.

1966 February 10. The state legislature ratified

the 25th Amendment to the United States Constitution.

1969   January 9. Deane C. Davis, Republican, who had beene elected in 1968, became governor of the state. He served in the office until January 4, 1973.

1970   Population: 444,330.

The state legislature passed a Land Use and Development Control Act. The law gave the state government the right to limit any proposal and development which might harm the environment.

1971   March 22. When the federal "Railpax" routes for the railroads were announced, Vermont was not on any route.

April 16. The state legislature ratified the 26th Amendment to the United States Constitution.

1972   January 14. The Vermont Supreme Court ruled in a unanimous decision that the state's 125-year-old abortion law was unconstitutional.

1973   January 4. Thomas P. Salmon, Democrat, who had been elected in 1972, became governor of the state. He was reelected in 1974 and served in the office until January 1977.

1974   March. The issue of the impeachment of President Richard M. Nixon was discussed at 13 annual town meetings in the state. Eight towns approved resolutions calling for his impeachment and five defeated or tabled the issue.

October 7. President Gerald R. Ford attended a Republican banquet at Burlington.

November 5. Governor Thomas P. Salmon was reelected.

1976   January 26. The Vermont Nuclear Power Corporation closed its 540,000 kilowatt nuclear generating plant in Vernon as a safety precaution.

October 2. Republican Vice Presidential

nominee, Senator Robert J. Dole, campaigned in Burlington.

November 2. Richard Snelling, Republican, was elected governor of the state.

1977   January. Richard Snelling was inaugurated as governor of Vermont.

January 21. Exiled Soviet author Alexander I. Solzhenitsyn announced his intention to start a nonprofit publishing company in Vermont. This company would distribute works on Russian culture, history and religion in the United States and abroad.

BIOGRAPHICAL DIRECTORY

The selected list of governors, United States Senators and Members of the House of Representatives for Vermont, 1789-1977, includes all persons listed in the Chronology for whom basic biographical data was readily available. Older biographical sources are frequently in conflict on certain individuals, and in such cases the source most commonly cited by later authorities was preferred.

BIOGRAPHICAL DIRECTORY   23

BUCK, Daniel
    Federalist
    b. Hebron, Conn., April 19, 1789
    d. Chelsea, Vt., December 8, 1841
    U. S. Representative, 1823-25, 1827-29

BUTLER, Ezra
    Democrat
    b. Lancaster, Mass., September 24, 1763
    d. Waterbury, Vt., September 24, 1763
    U. S. Representative, 1813-15
    Governor of Vermont, 1826-28

CAHOON, William
    Anti-Masonic
    b. Providence, R. I., January 12, 1774
    d. Lyndon, Vt., May 30, 1833
    U. S. Representative, 1829-33

CHAMBERLAIN, William
    Federalist
    b. Hopkinton, Mass., April 27, 1755
    d. Peacham, Vt., September 27, 1828
    U. S. Representative, 1803-05, 1809-11

CHASE, Dudley
    Jackson Democrat
    b. Cornish, N. H., December 30, 1771
    d. Randolph Center, Vt., February 23, 1846
    U. S. Senator, 1813-17, 1825-31

CHIPMAN, Daniel
    Federalist
    b. Salisbury, Conn., October 22, 1765
    d. Ripton, Vt., April 23, 1850
    U. S. Representative, 1815-16

CHIPMAN, Nathaniel
    ----
    b. Salisbury, Conn., November 15, 1752
    d. Tinmouth, Vt., January 15, 1843
    U. S. Senator, 1797-1803

CHITTENDEN, Martin
    ----
    b. Salisbury, Conn., March 12, 1763
    d. Williston, Vt., March 12, 1763
    U. S. Representative, 1803-13
    Governor of Vermont, 1814-15

CHITTENDEN, Thomas
    ----
    b. East Guilford, Conn., January 6, 1730

    d. Williston, Vt., August 25, 1797
    Governor of Vermont, 1790-97

CLEMENT, Percival Wood
    Republican
    b. Rutland, Vt., July 7, 1846
    d. January 9, 1927
    Governor of Vermont, 1919-21

COLLAMER, Jacob
    Republican
    b. Troy, N. Y., January 8, 1792
    d. Woodstock, Vt., November 9, 1865
    U. S. Representative, 1843-49 (Whig)
    U. S. Postmaster General, 1849-50
    U. S. Senator, 1855-65

CONVERSE, Julius
    Republican
    Governor of Vermont, 1872-74

COOLIDGE, Carlos
    Whig
    Governor of Vermont, 1848-50

CRAFTS, Samuel Chandler
    National Republican
    b. Woodstock, Conn., October 6, 1768
    d. Craftsbury, Vt., November 19, 1853
    U. S. Representative, 1817-25
    Governor of Vermont, 1828-31
    U. S. Senator, 1842-43

DALE, Porter Hinman
    Republican
    b. Island Pond, Vt., March 1, 1867
    d. at his summer home, Westmore, Vt.,
        October 6, 1933
    U. S. Representative, 1915-23
    U. S. Senator, 1923-33

DEMING, Benjamin F.
    Whig
    b. Danville, Vt., 1790
    d. Saratoga Springs, N. Y., July 11, 1834
    U. S. Representative, 1833-34

DENISON, Dudley Chase
    Republican
    b. Royalton, Vt., September 13, 1819
    d. Royalton, Vt., February 10, 1905
    U. S. Representative, 1875-79

DILLINGHAM, Paul, Jr.
　　Republican
　　b. Shutesbury, Mass., August 10, 1799
　　d. Waterbury, Vt., July 26, 1891
　　Governor of Vermont, 1865-67

DILLINGHAM, William Paul
　　Republican
　　b. Waterbury, Vt., December 12, 1843
　　d. Montpelier, Vt., July 12, 1923
　　Governor of Vermont, 1889-90
　　U. S. Senator, 1900-23

EATON, Horace
　　Whig
　　Governor of Vermont, 1846-48

EDMUNDS, George Franklin
　　Republican
　　b. Richmond, Vt., February 1, 1828
　　d. Pasadena, Calif., February 27, o919
　　U. S. Senator, 1866-91; President pro
　　　　tempore, 1883-85

ELLIOTT, James
　　Federalist
　　b. Gloucester, Mass., August 18, 1775
　　d. Newfame, Vt., November 10, 1839
　　U. S. Representative, 1803-09

EMERSON, Lee E.
　　Republican
　　Governor of Vermont, 1951-55

EVERETT, Horace
　　Whig
　　b. Foxboro, Mass., July 17, 1779
　　d. Windsor, Vt., January 30, 1851
　　U. S. Representative, 1829-43

FAIRBANKS, Erastus
　　Whig
　　b. Brimfield, Mass., October 28, 1797
　　d. St. Johnsbury, Vt., November 20, 1864
　　Governor of Vermont, 1852-53

FAIRBANKS, Horace
　　Republican
　　Governor of Vermont, 1876-78

FARNHAM, Roswell
　　Republican
　　b. Boston, Mass., July 23, 1827

d. 1903
Governor of Vermont, 1880-82

FISK, James
   Democrat
   b. Greenwich, Mass., October 4, 1763
   d. Swanton, Vt., November 17, 1844
   U. S. Representative, 1805-09, 1811-15
   U. S. Senator, 1817-18

FLANDERS, Ralph Edward
   Republican
   b. Barnet, Vt., September 28, 1880
   d. Springfield, Vt., February 19, 1870
   U. S. Senator, 1846-59

FLEETWOOD, Frederick Gleed
   Republican
   b. St. Johnsbury, Vt., September 27, 1868
   d. Morrisville, Vt., January 28, 1938
   U. S. Representative, 1923-25

FLETCHER, Allen M.
   Republican
   Governor of Vermont, 1912-15

FLETCHER, Isaac
   Anti-Masonic Democrat
   b. Dunstable, Mass., November 22, 1784
   d. Lyndon, Vt., October 19, 1842
   U. S. Representative, 1837-41

FLETCHER, Ryland
   Republican
   Governor of Vermont, 1856-58

FOOT, Solomon
   Republican
   b. Cornwall, Vt., November 19, 1802
   d. Washington, D. C., March 28, 1866
   U. S. Representative, 1843-47 (Whig)
   U. S. Senator, 1851-57 (Whig), 1857-66
     (Republican): President pro tempore,
     1860-64

FOSTER, David Johnson
   Republican
   b. Barnet, Vt., June 27, 1857
   d. Washington, D. C., March 21, 1912
   U. S. Representative, 1901-12

FULLER, Levi K.
   Republican

Governor of Vermont, 1892-94

GALUSHA, Jonas
    Democrat-Republican
    Governor of Vermont, 1809-13, 1815-20

GATES, Charles Winslow
    Republican
    b. Franklin, Vt., January 12, 1856
    d. July 1, 1927
    Governor of Vermont, 1915-17

GIBSON, Ernest Willard
    Republican
    b. Londonderry, Vt., December 29, 1872
    d. Washington, D. C., June 20, 1940
    U. S. Representative, 1923-33
    U. S. Senator, 1933-40

GIBSON, Ernest William
    Republican
    b. Brattleboro, Vt., March 6, 1901
    d. Brattleboro, Vt., November 4, 1969
    U. S. Senator, 1940-41
    Governor of Vermont, 1947-50

GRAHAM, Horace French
    Republican
    b. New York, N. Y., February 7, 1862
    d. November 23, 1941
    Governor of Vermont, 1917-19

GREENE, Frank Lester
    Republican
    b. St. Albans, Vt., February 10, 1870
    d. St. Albans, Vt., December 17, 1930
    U. S. Representative, 1917-23
    U. S. Senator, 1923-30

GROUT, Josiah
    Republican
    b. Compton, Quebec, Canada, May 28, 1841
    d. July 19, 1925
    Governor of Vermont, 1896-98

GROUT, William Wallace
    Republican
    b. Crompton, Quebec, Canada, May 24, 1836
    d. Kirby, Vt., October 7, 1902
    U. S. Representative, 1881-83, 1885-1901

HALL, Hiland
    Whig

b. Bennington, Vt., July 20, 1795
   d. Springfield, Mass., December 18, 1885
   U. S. Representative, 1833-43
   Governor of Vermont, 1858-60

HARTNESS, James
   Republican
   b. Schenectady, N. Y., September 3, 1861
   d. February 2, 1934
   Governor of Vermont, 1921-23

HASKINS, Kittredge
   Republican
   b. Dover, Vt., April 8, 1836
   d. Brattleboro, Vt., August 7, 1916
   U. S. Representative, 1901-09

HEBARD, William
   Whig
   b. Windham, Conn., November 29, 1800
   d. Chelsea, Vt., October 20, 1875
   U. S. Representative, 1849-53

HENDEE, George Whitman
   Republican
   b. Stowe, Vt., November 30, 1882
   d. Morrisville, Vt., December 6, 1906
   Governor of Vermont, 1870
   U. S. Representative, 1873-79

HENRY, William
   Whig
   b. Charlestown, N. H., March 22, 1788
   d. Bellows Falls, Vt., April 16, 1861
   U. S. Representative, 1847-51

HODGES, George Tirdale
   Republican
   b. Clarendon, Vt., July 4, 1789
   d. Rutland, Vt., August 9, 1860
   U. S. Representative, 1856-57

HOFF, Phillip H.
   Democrat
   b. Greenfield, Mass., June 29, 1924
   Governor of Vermont, 1963-69

HOLBROOK, Frederick
   Republican
   b. Warehouse Point, Conn., February 15,
      1813
   d. 1909
   Governor of Vermont, 1861-63

HUBBARD, Jonathan Hatch
    Federalist
    b. Tolland, Conn., May 7, 1768
    d. Windsor, Vt., September 20, 1849
    U. S. Representative, 1809-11

HUNT, Jonathan
    National Republican
    b. Vernon, Vt., August 12, 1787
    d. Washington, D. C., May 15, 1932
    U. S. Representative, 1827-32

HUNTER, William
    Republican
    b. Sheron, Conn., January 3, 1754
    d. Windsor, Vt., November 30, 1827
    U. S. Representative, 1817-19

JANES, Henry Fisk
    Whig/Anti-Monopolist
    b. Brimfield, Mass., October 10, 1792
    d. Waterbury, Vt., June 6, 1879
    U. S. Representative, 1834-37

JENNISON, Silas H.
    Whig
    Governor of Vermont, 1835-41

JEWETT, Luther
    Federalist
    b. Canterbury, Conn., December 24, 1772
    d. St. Johnsbury, Vt., March 8, 1860
    U. S. Representative, 1815-17

JOHNSON, Joseph Blaine
    Republican
    b. Helsingborg, Sweden, August 29, 1893
    Governor of Vermont, 1955-59

JOYCE, Charles Herbert
    Republican
    b. near Andover, England, January 30,
        1830
    d. Pittsfield, Vt., November 22, 1916
    U. S. Representative, 1875-83

KEYES, Elias
    Republican
    b. Ashford, Conn., April 14, 1758
    d. Stockbridge, Vt., July 9, 1844
    U. S. Representative, 1821-23

KEYSER, Frank Ray, Jr.

Republican
b. Chelsea, Vt., August 17, 1927
Governor of Vermont, 1961-63

LANGDON, Chauncey
　Federalist
　b. Farmington, Conn., November 8, 1763
　d. Castleton, Vt., July 23, 1830
　U. S. Representative, 1815-17

LYON, Asa
　Federalist
　b. Pomfret, Conn., December 31, 1763
　d. South Hero, Vt., April 8, 1841
　U. S. Representative, 1815-17

MALLARY, Rollin Carolas
　----
　b. Cheshire, Conn., May 27, 1784
　d. Baltimore, Vt., April 16, 1831
　U. S. Representative, 1820-31

MARSH, Charles
　Federalist
　b. Lebanon, Conn., July 10, 1765
　d. Woodstock, Vt., January 11, 1849
　U. S. Representative, 1815-17

MARSH, George Perkins
　Whig
　b. Woodstock, Vt., March 15, 1801
　d. Vallambrosa, Italy, July 24, 1882
　U. S. Representative, 1843-49

MATTOCKS, John
　Whig
　b. Hartford, Conn., March 4, 1777
　d. Peacham, Vt., August 14, 1847
　U. S. Representative, 1821-23, 1825-27,
　　　1841-43
　Governor of Vermont, 1843-44

MCCULLOUGH, John Griffith
　Republican
　b. on Welch Tract, near Newark, Del.,
　　　September 16, 1835
　d. May 29, 1915
　Governor of Vermont, 1902-04

MEACHAM, James
　Whig
　b. Rutland, Vt., August 16, 1810

d. Rutland, Vt., August 23, 1856
U. S. Representative, 1849-56

MEAD, John Abner
    Republican
    b. Fairhaven, Vt., April 20, 1841
    d. January 12, 1920
    Governor of Vermont, 1910-12

MEECH, Ezra
    Democrat
    b. New London, Conn., July 26, 1773
    d. Shelburne, Vt., September 23, 1856
    U. S. Representative, 1819-21, 1825-27

MERRILL, Orasmus Cook
    Democrat
    b. Falmington, Conn., June 18, 1775
    d. Bennington, Vt., April 12, 1865
    U. S. Representative, 1817-20

MEYER, William Henry
    Democrat
    b. Philadelphia, Pa., December 29, 1914
    U. S. Representative, 1959-61

MINER, Ahiman Louis
    Whig
    b. Middletown, Vt., September 23, 1804
    d. Manchester, Vt., July 19, 1886
    U. S. Representative, 1851-53

MORRILL, Justin Smith
    Union Republican
    b. Strafford, Vt., April 14, 1810
    d. Washington, Vt., December 28, 1898
    U. S. Representative, 1855-67 (Whig)
    U. S. Senator, 1867-98

MORRIS, Lewis Robert
    Federalist
    b. Scarsdale, N. Y., November 2, 1760
    d. Springfield, Vt., December 29, 1825
    U. S. Representative, 1797-1803

NILES, Nathaniel
    ----
    b. South Kingston, R. I., April 3, 1741
    d. Fairlee, Vt., October 31, 1828
    U. S. Representative, 1791-95

OLIN, Gideon
    Democrat

VERMONT

    b. East Greenwich, R. I., November 2, 1743
    d. Shaftesbury, Vt., January 21, 1823
    U. S. Representative, 1803-07

OLIN, Henry
    Jefferson Democrat
    b. Shaftsbury, Vt., May 7, 1768
    d. Salisbury, Vt., August 16, 1937
    U. S. Representative, 1824-25

ORMSBEE, Ebenezer Jolls
    Republican
    b. Snoreham, Vt., June 8, 1834
    d. April 3, 1924
    Governor of Vermont, 1886-88

PAGE, Carroll Smalley
    Republican
    b. Westfield, Vt., January 10, 1843
    d. Hyde Park, Vt., December 3, 1925
    Governor of Vermont, 1890-92
    U. S. Senator, 1908-23

PAGE, John B.
    Republican
    Governor of Vermont, 1867-69

PAINE, Charles
    Whig
    b. Williamston, Vt., April 15, 1799
    d. while on an inspection tour for a proposed Pacific route through the Southwest at Waco, Texas, July 6, 1853
    Governor of Vermont, 1841-43

PAINE, Elijah
    Federalist
    b. Brooklyn, Conn., January 21, 1757
    d. Williamston, Vt., April 28, 1842
    U. S. Senator, 1795-1801

PALMER, William Adams
    Democrat
    b. Hebron, Conn., September 12, 1781
    d. Danville, Vt., December 3, 1860
    U. S. Senator, 1818-25
    Governor of Vermont, 1831-35

PARTRIDGE, Frank Charles
    Republican
    b. East Middlebury, Vt., May 7, 1861
    d. Proctor, Vt., March 2, 1943
    U. S. Senator, 1930-31

PECK, Asahel
    Republican
    Governor of Vermont, 1874-76

PECK, Lucius Benedict
    Democrat
    b. Waterbury, Vt., November 17, 1802
    d. Lowell, Mass., December 28, 1866
    U. S. Representative, 1847-51

PHELPS, Samuel Shethar
    Whig
    b. Litchfield, Conn., May 13, 1793
    d. Middlebury, Vt., March 25, 1855
    U. S. Senator, 1839-51, 1853-54

PINGREE, Samuel Everett
    Republican
    b. Salisbury, N. H., August 2, 1832
    d. June 1, 1922
    Governor of Vermont, 1884-86

PLUMLEY, Charles Albert
    Republican
    b. Northfield, Vt., April 14, 1875
    d. Barre, Vt., October 31, 1964
    U. S. Representative, 1934-51

PLUMLEY, Frank
    Republican
    b. Eden, Vt., December 17, 1844
    d. Northfield, Vt., April 30, 1924
    U. S. Representative, 1909-15

POLAND, Luke Potter
    Republican
    b. Westford, Vt., November 1, 1813
    d. at his country home near Waterville,
        Vt., July 2, 1887
    U. S. Senator, 1865-67
    U. S. Representative, 1867-75, 1883-85

POWERS, Horace Henry
    Republican
    b. Morristown, Vt., May 29, 1835
    d. Morrisville, Vt., December 8, 1913
    U. S. Representative, 1891-1901

PRENTISS, Samuel
    Whig
    b. Stonington, Conn., March 31, 1782
    d. Montpelier, Vt., January 15, 1857
    U. S. Senator, 1831-42

PROCTOR, Fletcher Dutton
    Republican
    b. Cavendish, Vt., November 7, 1860
    d. 1911
    Governor of Vermont, 1906-08

PROCTOR, Mortimer Robinson
    Republican
    b. Proctor, Vt., May 30, 1889
    d. April 28, 1968
    Governor of Vermont, 1945-47

PROCTOR, Redfield
    Republican
    b. Proctorville, Vt., June 1, 1831
    d. Washington, D. C., March 4, 1903
    Governor of Vermont, 1878-80
    U. S. Secretary of War, 1889-91
    U. S. Senator, 1891-1908

PROCTOR, Redfield
    Republican
    b. Proctor, Vt., April 13, 1879
    d. February 5, 1957
    Governor of Vermont, 1923-25

PROUTY, George Herbert
    Republican
    b. Newport, Vt., March 4, 1862
    d. August 19, 1918
    Governor of Vermont, 1908-10

PROUTY, Winston Lewis
    Republican
    b. Newport, Vt., September 1, 1906
    d. Boston, Mass., September 10, 1971
    U. S. Representative, 1951-59
    U. S. Senator, 1959-71

RICHARDS, Mark
    Democrat
    b. Waterbury, Conn., July 15, 1760
    d. Westminster, Vt., August 10, 1844
    U. S. Representative, 1817-21

ROBINSON, John S.
    Democrat
    Governor of Vermont, 1853-54

ROBINSON, Jonathan
    ----
    b. Hardwick, Mass., August 11, 1756
    d. Bennington, Vt., November 3, 1819

U. S. Senator, 1807-15

ROBINSON, Moses
    Democrat
    b. Hardwick, Mass., March 20, 1741
    d. Bennington, Vt., May 26, 1813
    Governor of Vermont, 1789-90
    U. S. Senator, 1791-96

ROSS, Jonathan
    Republican
    b. Waterford, Vt., April 30, 1826
    d. St. Johnsbury, Vt., February 23, 1905
    U. S. Senator, 1899-1900

ROYCE, Homer Elihu
    Republican
    b. East Berkshire, Vt., June 14, 1819
    d. St. Albans, Vt., April 24, 1891
    U. S. Representative, 1857-61

ROYCE, Stephen
    Whig/Republican
    Governor of Vermont, 1854-66

SABIN, Alvah
    Whig
    b. Georgia, Vt., October 23, 1793
    d. Sycamore, Ill., January 22, 1885
    U. S. Representative, 1853-57

SALMON, Thomas Paul
    Democrat
    b. Cleveland, Ohio, August 19, 1932
    Governor of Vermont, 1973-

SEYMOUR, Horatio
    Clay Democrat
    b. Litchfield, Conn., May 31, 1778
    d. Middlebury, Vt., November 21, 1857
    U. S. Senator, 1821-33

SHAW, Samuel
    Democrat
    b. Dighton, Mass., December 1763
    d. Clarendon Springs, Vt., October 23, 1827
    U. S. Representative, 1808-13

SKINNER, Richard
    Democrat
    b. Litchfield, Conn., May 30, 1778
    d. Manchester, Vt., May 23, 1833
    U. S. Representative, 1813-15

Governor of Vermont, 1820-23

SLADE, William
　Whig
　b. Cornwall, Vt., May 9, 1786
　d. Middlebury, Vt., January 18, 1859
　U. S. Representative, 1831-43
　Governor of Vermont, 1844-46

SMITH, Edward Curtis
　Republican
　b. St. Albans, Vt., January 5, 1854
　d. April 6, 1935
　Governor of Vermont, 1898-1900

SMITH, Israel
　Democrat
　b. Suffield, Conn., April 4, 1759
　d. Rutland, Vt., December 2, 1810
　U. S. Representative, 1791-97, 1801-03
　U. S. Senator, 1803-07
　Governor of Vermont, 1807-08

SMITH, John
　Democrat
　b. Barre, Mass., August 12, 1789
　d. St. Albans, Vt., November 26, 1858
　U. S. Representative, 1839-41

SMITH, John Gregory
　Republican
　b. St. Albans, Vt., July 22, 1818
　d. St. Albans, Vt., November 6, 1891
　Governor of Vermont, 1863-65

SMITH, Worthington Curtis
　Republican
　b. St. Albans, Vt., April 23, 1823
　d. St. Albans, Vt., January 2, 1894
　U. S. Representative, 1867-73

STAFFORD, Robert Theodore
　Republican
　b. Rutland, Vt., August 8, 1913
　Governor of Vermont, 1959-61
　U. S. Representative, 1961-

STEWART, John Wolcott
　Republican
　b. Middlebury, Vt., November 24, 1825
　d. Middlebury, Vt., October 29, 1915
　Governor of Vermont, 1870-72
　U. S. Representative, 1883-91

U. S. Senator, 1908

STICKNEY, William Wallace
    Republican
    b. Plymouth, Vt., March 21, 1853
    d. December 15, 1932
    Governor of Vermont, 1900-02

STRONG, William
    Democrat
    b. Lebanon, Conn., 1763
    d. Hartford, Vt., January 28, 1840
    U. S. Representative, 1811-15, 1819-21

SWIFT, Benjamin
    Federalist
    b. Amenia, N. Y., April 3, 1781
    d. St. Albans, Vt., November 11, 1847
    U. S. Representative, 1827-31
    U. S. Senator, 1833-39

TICHENOR, Isaac
    Federalist
    b. Newark, N. J., February 8, 1754
    d. Bennington, Vt., December 11, 1838
    U. S. Senator, 1796-97
    Governor of Vermont, 1797-1806, 1808
    U. S. Senator, 1815-21

TRACY, Andrew
    Whig
    b. Hartford, Vt., December 15, 1797
    d. Woodstock, Vt., October 28, 1868
    U. S. Representative, 1853-55

TYLER, James Manning
    Republican
    b. Wilmington, Vt., April 27, 1835
    d. Bratt;eboro, Vt., October 13, 1926
    U. S. Representative, 1879-83

UPHAM, William
    Whig
    b. Leicester, Mass., August 5, 1792
    d. Washington, D. C., January 14, 1853
    U. S. Senator, 1843-53

VAN NESS, Cornelius P.
    Democrat-Republican
    Governor of Vermont, 1823-26

WALES, George Edward
    ----
    b. Westminster, Vt., May 13, 1792
    d. Hartford, Vt., January 8, 1866
    U. S. Representative, 1825-29

WALTON, Eliakim Persons
    Republican
    b. Montpelier, Vt., February 17, 1812
    d. Montpelier, Vt., December 19, 1890
    U. S. Representative, 1857-63

WASHBURN, Peter Thacher
    Republican
    b. Lynn, Mass., September 7, 1814
    d. Woodstock, Vt., February 7, 1870
    Governor of Vermont, 1869-70

WEEKS, John Eliakim
    Republican
    b. Salisbury, Vt., June 14, 1853
    d. Middlebury, Vt., September 10, 1949
    Governor of Vermont, 1927-31
    U. S. Representative, 1931-33

WHITE, Phineas
    Democrat
    b. South Hadley, Mass., October 30, 1770
    d. Putney, Vt., July 6, 1847
    U. S. Representative, 1821-23

WILLARD, Charles Wesley
    Republican
    b. Lyndon, Vt., June 18, 1827
    d. Montpelier, Vt., June 8, 1880
    U. S. Representative, 1869-75

WILLIAMS, Charles K.
    Whig
    Governor of Vermont, 1850-52

WILLS, William Henry
    Republican
    b. Chicago, Ill., October 26, 1882
    d. March 6, 1946
    Governor of Vermont, 1941-45

WILSON, Stanley Calef
    Republican
    b. Orange, Vt., September 10, 1879
    d. ----
    Governor of Vermont, 1931-35

WITHERELL, James
    Democrat
    b. Mansfield, Mass., June 16, 1759
    d. Detroit, Mich., January 9, 1838
    U. S. Representative, 1807-08

WOODBRIDGE, Frederick Enoch
    Republican
    b. Vergennes, Vt., August 29, 1818
    d. Vergennes, Vt., April 25, 1888
    U. S. Representative, 1863-69

WOODBURY, Urban Andrain
    Republican
    b. Acworth, N. H., July 11, 1838
    d. April 15, 1915
    Governor of Vermont, 1894-96

YOUNG, Augustus
    Whig
    b. Arlington, Vt., March 20, 1784
    d. St. Albans, Vt., June 17, 1857
    U. S. Representative, 1841-43

PROMINENT PERSONALITIES

The following select list of prominent persons of Vermont has been selected to indicate the valuable contributions they have made to American life.

PROMINENT PERSONALITIES

ALLEN, Ethan
    b. January 21, 1738
    d. February 2, 1789
    Served in French and Indian War, 1757
    Colonel, Green Mountain Boys, 1770
    Captured Fort Ticonderoga, 1775
    Brevetted Colonel, Continental Army by
        General George Washington, 1778
    Author: *1779: A Narrative of Col. Ethan Allen's
        Captivity*

ALLEN, Ira
    b. May 1, 1751
    d. January 15, 1814
    Member Vermont Governor's Council, 1777
    First Treasurer of Vermont, 1778
    Author: *Natural and Political History of
        the State of Vermont*, 1798

COOLIDGE, Calvin
    b. Plymouth, Vt., July 4, 1872
    d. January 5, 1933
    Lieutenant Governor of Massachusetts, 1916,
        1917, 1918
    Governor of Massachusetts, 1919, 1920
    Vice President of the United States, 1921-
        23
    30th President of the United States, 1923-
        29

DAVENPORT, Thomas
    b. Williamstown, Vt., July 9, 1802
    d. July 6, 1851
    Built small circular railway (first recorded
        electric railway), 1835
    Invented early model of electric train
        motor, 1836

DEWEY, George
    b. Montpelier, Vt., December 26, 1837
    d. January 16, 1917
    Graduate U. S. Naval Academy, 1858
    Destroyed Spanish fleet in Battle of Manila
        Bay and aided army in capture of
        City of Manila, Phillipine Islands,
        1898
    Admiral, U. S. Navy, 1899-1917
    President, General Board, U. S. Navy
        Department, Washington, D. C., 1900-17

DEWEY, John
  b. Burlington, Vt., October 20, 1859
  d. June 2, 1952
  Professor, University of Minnesota, 1888-89
  Professor, University of Michigan, 1889-94
  Professor, University of Chicago, 1894-1904
  Professor, Columbia University, 1904-52
  Author: *School and Society*, 1899
        How We Think, 1909
        Art As Experience, 1934
        Logic: The Theory of Inquiry, 1938

FAIRBANKS, Thaddeus
  b. Brimfield, Mass., January 17, 1796
  d. April 12, 1886
  Devised first platform scale - obtained basic patent, 1831
  Partner in E. and T. Fairbanks and Company, manufacturer of Platform scales
  Established St. Johnsbury Academy, 1842
  Invented hot water heater, 1881

FAY, Jonas
  b. Westborough, Mass., January 28, 1737
  d. March 6, 1818
  Surgeon to Green Mountain Boys, 1775
  Member Windsor Convention - drafted Vermont Constitution
  Judge, Supreme Court of Vermont, 1782
  Judge Probate Court, 1782-87
  Author: *A Concise Refutation of the Claims of New Hampshire and Massachusetts Bay to the Territory of Vermont* (with Ethan Allen), 1780

MEAD, Larkin Goldsmith
  b. Chesterfield, N. H., January 3, 1835
  d. 1910
  Sculptor
  Attached to U. S. Consulate at Venice
  Artist for *Harper's Weekly*, Civil War
  Works: National Lincoln Monument, Springfield, Ill.
      Soldiers' Monument, St. Johnsbury, Vt.

HALL, Samuel Read
  b. Croydon, N. H., October 27, 1795
  d. June 24, 1877
  Credited with first use of blackboards in United States
  Established first normal school in United

PROMINENT PERSONALITIES

States - teachers college, 1823
Founder of American Institute of Instruction,
Boston - oldest educational association
in U. S., 1830
Principal, Phillips Academy Andover, Mass.,
1830-37

MARSH, James
b. Hartford, Vt., July 19, 1794
d. Burlington, Vt., July 3, 1842
President, University of Vermont, Burlington, 1826-33
Editor, Aid to Reflection, 1829

MAYO, Henry Thomas
b. Burlington, Vt., December 8, 1856
d. February 23, 1937
U. S. Admiral, 1916
Commander-in-chief, Atlantic Fleet, U. S. Navy, 1917-19

MORTON, Levi Parsons
b. Shoreham, Vt., May 16, 1824
d. Rhinebeck, N. Y., May 16, 1920
U. S. Representative (New York), 1879-81
Vice President of the United States, 1889-93
Governor of New York, 1895-96

ROBINSON, Rowland Evans
b. Ferrisburgh, Vt., May 14, 1833
d. 1900
Author: Danvis Folks
Uncle 'Lisha's Shop
In New England Fields and Woods
Uncle 'Lisha's Outing
A Hero of Ticonderoga
Sam Lovell's Camps
Vermont: A Study of Independence

ROCKWELL, Norman
b. New York, N. Y., February 3, 1894
Painter of magazine covers and illustrations, mainly for Saturday Evening Post - also Ladies Home Journal, American Magazine, Woman's Home Companion, Look Magazine, McCall's Magazine

SARGENT, John G.
b. Ludlow, Vt., October 13, 1860
d. March 5, 1939
Attorney General of Vermont, 1908-12
U. S. Attorney General, 1925-29

SMITH, Joseph
    b. Sharon, Vt., December 23, 1805
    d. when shot by a mob, Carthage, Ill.,
        June 27, 1844
    Received visions, 1820-27 - revealed was
        selected to restore Church of Christ
        to earth
    Author: *The Book of Mormon*, 1830
    Founder, Church of Jesus Christ of Latter-
        Day Saints, Fayette, N. Y., 1830
    Removed community to Kirtland, Ohio, 1831,
        Jackson County, Mo., 1838, Commerce
        (renamed Nauvoo), Ill., 1839

TAFT, Alphonso
    b. Townsend, Vt., November 5, 1810
    d. San Diego, Calif., May 21, 1891
    Judge, Cincinnati Superior Court, 1865-72
    U. S. Secretary of War, 1876
    U. S. Attorney General, 1876-77
    U. S. Minister to Austria-Hungary, 1882-84
    U. S. Minister to Russia, 1884-85

THOMPSON, Daniel Pierce
    b. Charlestown, Mass., October 1, 1795
    d, Montpelier, Vt., June 6, 1868
    Judge, Probate Court for Washington County,
        1837-40, 1841-42
    Member Vermont Supreme Court, 1843-45
    Vermont Secretary of State, 1853-55

WARNER, Seth
    b. Roxbury, Conn., April 25, 1795
    d. Roxbury, Conn, December 26, 1784
    Led force to seize Crown Point, 1775
    Lieutenant colonel, Vermont regiment, 1775
    Fought Battle of Bennington, August 16, 1777
    Commissioned Brigadier General by Vermont
        Assembly, 1778

FIRST STATE CONSTITUTION

VERMONT[a]

CONSTITUTION OF VERMONT—1777 [*][b]

WHEREAS, all government ought to be instituted and supported, for the security and protection of the community, as such, and to enable the individuals who compose it, to enjoy their natural rights, and the other blessings which the Author of existence has bestowed upon man; and whenever those great ends of government are not obtained, the people have a right, by common consent, to change it, and take such measures as to them may appear necessary to promote their safety and happiness.

And whereas, the inhabitants of this State have (in consideration of protection only) heretofore acknowledged allegiance to the King of Great Britain, and the said King has not only withdrawn that protection, but commenced, and still continues to carry on, with unabated vengeance, a most cruel and unjust war against them; employing therein, not only the troops of Great Britain, but foreign mercenaries, savages and slaves, for the avowed purpose of reducing them to a total and abject submission to the despotic domination of the British parliament, with many other acts of tyranny, (more fully set forth in the declaration of Congress) whereby all allegiance and fealty to the said King and his successors, are dissolved and at an end; and all power and authority derived from him, ceased in the American Colonies.

---

[*] Verified from "Vermont State Papers; Being a Collection of Records and Documents, Connected with the Assumption and Establishment of Government by the People of Vermont; together with the Journal of the Council of Safety, the First Constitution, the early Journals of the General Assembly, and the Laws from the year 1779 to 1786, inclusive. To which are added the Proceedings of the First and Second Councils of Censors. Compiled and Published by William Slade Jun. Secretary of State, Middlebury: J. W. Copeland, Printer. 1823." pp. 241-255.

[a] The State of Vermont was originally claimed by Massachusetts, New Hampshire, and New York, and at the commencement of the revolutionary struggle she not only sought independence from British rule, but from the State of New York, which claimed sovereignty over the territory to the west bank of the Connecticut River, and from New Hampshire, which contested the claims of both New York and Vermont. In March, 1781, Massachusetts assented to the independence of Vermont, which adjusted her difficulties with New Hampshire in 1782, but it was 1790 before New York consented to her admission into the Union.

[b] This constitution was framed by a convention which assembled at Windsor, July 2, 1777, and completed its labors July 8, 1777. It was not submitted to the people for ratification. It was affirmed by the legislature at its sessions in 1779 and 1782, and declared to be a part of the laws of the State. The convention subsequently met, on December 24, 1777, after the time of election and the day of meeting of the Assembly.

And whereas, the territory which now comprehends the State of *Vermont*, did antecedently, of right, belong to the government of *New-Hampshire;* and the former Governor thereof, viz. his Excellency *Benning Wentworth*, Esq., granted many charters of lands and corporations, within this State, to the present inhabitants and others. And whereas, the late Lieutenant Governor *Colden*, of *New York*, with others, did, in violation of the tenth command, covet those very lands; and by a false representation made to the court of Great Britain, (in the year 1764, that for the convenience of trade and administration of justice, the inhabitants were desirous of being annexed to that government,) obtained jurisdiction of those very identical lands, *ex-parte;* which ever was, and is, disagreeable to the inhabitants. And whereas, the legislautre of *New-York*, ever have, and still continue to disown the good people of this State, in their landed property, which will appear in the complaints hereafter inserted, and in the 36th section of their present constitution, in which is established the grants of land made by that government.

They have refused to make regrants of our lands to the original proprietors and occupants, unless at the exorbitant rate of 2300 dollars fees for each township; and did enhance the quit-rent, three fold, and demanded an immediate delivery of the title derived before, from *New-Hampshire.*

The judges of their supreme court have made a solemn declaration, that the charters, conveyances, &c. of the lands included in the before described premises, were utterly null and void, on which said title was founded: in consequence of which declaration, writs of possession have been by them issued, and the sheriff of the county of Albany sent, at the head of six or seven hundred men, to enforce the execution thereof.

They have passed an act, annexing a penalty thereto, of thirty pounds fine and six months imprisonment, on any person who should refuse assisting the sheriff, after being requested, for the purpose of executing writs of possession.

The Governors, *Dunmore, Tryon* and *Colden*, have made re-grants of several tracts of land, included in the premises, to certain favorite land jobbers in the government of *New-York*, in direct violation of his Britannic majesty's express prohibition, in the year 1767.

They have issued proclamations, wherein they have offered large sums of money, for the purpose of apprehending those very persons who have dared boldly, and publicly, to appear in defence of their just rights.

They did pass twelve acts of outlawry, on the 9th day of March, A. D. 1774, impowering the respective judges of their supreme court, to award execution of death against those inhabitants in said district, that they should judge to be offenders, without trial.

They have, and still continue, an unjust claim to those lands, which greatly retards emigration into, and the settlement of, this State.

They have hired foreign troops, emigrants from *Scotland*, at two different times, and armed them, to drive us out of possession.

They have sent the savages on our frontiers, to distress us.

They have proceeded to erect the counties of Cumberland and Glocester, and establish courts of justice there, after they were discountenanced by the authority of Great Britain.

The free convention of the State of *New-York*, at *Harlem*, in the year 1776, unanimously voted, " That all quit-rents, formerly due to the King of Great Britain, are now due and owing to this Convention, or such future government as shall be hereafter established in this State."

In the several stages of the aforesaid oppressions, we have petitioned his Britannic majesty, in the most humble manner, for redress, and have, at very great expense, received several reports in our favor; and, in other instances, wherein we have petitioned the late legislative authority of *New-York*, those petitions have been treated with neglect.

And whereas, the local situation of this State, from *New-York*, at the extreme part, is upward of four hundred and fifty miles from the seat of that government, which renders it extreme difficult to continue under the jurisdiction of said State.

Therefore, it is absolutely necessary, for the welfare and safety of the inhabitants of this State, that it should be, henceforth, a free and independent State; and that a just, permanent, and proper form of government, should exist in it, derived from, and founded on, the authority of the people only, agreeable to the direction of the honorable American Congress.

We the representatives of the freemen of *Vermont*, in General Convention met, for the express purpose of forming such a government,— confessing the goodness of the Great Governor of the universe, (who alone, knows to what degree of earthly happiness, mankind may attain, by perfecting the arts of government,) in permitting the people of this State, by common consent, and without violence, deliberately to form for themselves, such just rules as they shall think best for governing their future society; and being fully convinced that it is our indispensable duty, to establish such original principles of government, as will best promote the general happiness of the people of this State, and their posterity, and provide for future improvements, without partiality for, or prejudice against, any particular class, sect, or denomination of men whatever,—do, by virtue of authority vested in us, by our constituents, ordain, declare, and establish, the following declaration of rights, and frame of government, to be the CONSTITUTION of this COMMONWEALTH, and to remain in force therein, forever, unaltered, except in such articles, as shall, hereafter, on experience, be found to require improvement, and which shall, by the same authority of the people, fairly delegated, as this frame of government directs, be amended or improved, for the more effectual obtaining and securing the great end and design of all government, herein before mentioned.

CHAPTER I

A DECLARATION OF THE RIGHTS OF THE INHABITANTS OF THE STATE OF VERMONT

I. THAT all men are born equally free and independent, and have certain natural, inherent and unalienable rights, amongst which are the enjoying and defending life and liberty; acquiring, possessing and protecting property, and pursuing and obtaining happiness and safety. Therefore, no male person, born in this country, or brought from over sea, ought to be holden by law, to serve any person, as a servant, slave or apprentice, after he arrives to the age of twenty-one years, nor female, in like manner, after she arrives to the age of eighteen years, unless they are bound by their own consent, after they arrive to such age, or bound by law, for the payment of debts, damages, fines, costs, or the like.

II. That private property ought to be subservient to public uses, when necessity requires it; nevertheless, whenever any particular man's property is taken for the use of the public, the owner ought to receive an equivalent in money.

III. That all men have a natural and unalienable right to worship ALMIGHTY GOD, according to the dictates of their own consciences and understanding, regulated by the word of GOD; and that no man ought, or of right can be compelled to attend any religious worship, or erect, or support any place of worship, or maintain any minister, contrary to the dictates of his conscience; nor can any man who professes the protestant religion, be justly deprived or abridged of any civil right, as a citizen, on account of his religious sentiment, or peculiar mode of religious worship, and that no authority can, or ought to be vested in, or assumed by, any power whatsoever, that shall, in any case, interfere with, or in any manner controul, the rights of conscience, in the free exercise of religious worship: nevertheless, every sect or denomination of people ought to observe the Sabbath, or the Lord's day, and keep up, and support, some sort of religious worship, which to them shall seem most agreeable to the revealed will of GOD.

IV. That the people of this State have the sole, exclusive and inherent right of governing and regulating the internal police of the same.

V. That all power being originally inherent in, and consequently, derived from, the people; therefore, all officers of government, whether legislative or executive, are their trustees and servants, and at all times accountable to them.

VI. That government is, or ought to be, instituted for the common benefit, protection, and security of the people, nation or community; and not for the particular emolument or advantage of any single man, family or set of men, who are a part only of that community; and that the community hath an indubitable, unalienable and indefeasible right to reform, alter, or abolish, government, in such manner as shall be, by that community, judged most conducive to the public weal.

VII. That those who are employed in the legislative and executive business of the State, may be restrained from oppression, the people have a right, at such periods as they may think proper, to reduce their public officers to a private station, and supply the vacancies by certain and regular elections.

VIII. That all elections ought to be free; and that all freemen, having a sufficient, evident, common interest with, and attachment to, the community, have a right to elect officers, or be elected into office.

IX. That every member of society hath a right to be protected in the enjoyment of life, liberty and property, and therefore, is bound to contribute his proportion towards the expense of that protection, and yield his personal service, when necessary, or an equivalent thereto; but no part of a man's property can be justly taken from him, or applied to public uses, without his own consent, or that of his legal representatives; nor can any man who is conscientiously scrupulous of bearing arms, be justly compelled thereto, if he will pay such equivalent; nor are the people bound by any law, but such as they have, in like manner, assented to, for their common good.

X. That, in all prosecutions for criminal offences, a man hath a right to be heard, by himself and his counsel—to demand the cause and nature of his accusation—to be confronted with the witnesses—to call for evidence in his favor, and a speedy public trial, by an impartial jury of the country; without the unanimous consent of which jury, he cannot be found guilty; nor can he be compelled to give evidence against himself; nor can any man be justly deprived of his liberty, except by the laws of the land or the judgment of his peers.

XI. That the people have a right to hold themselves, their houses, papers and possessions free from search or seizure; and therefore warrants, without oaths or affirmations first made, affording a sufficient foundation for them, and whereby any officer or messenger may be commanded or required to search suspected places, or to seize any person or persons, his, her or their property, not particularly described, are contrary to that right, and ought not to be granted.

XII. That no warrant or writ to attach the person or estate, of any freeholder within this State, shall be issued in civil action, without the person or persons, who may request such warrant or attachment, first make oath, or affirm, before the authority who may be requested to issue the same, that he, or they, are in danger of losing his, her or their debts.

XIII. That, in controversies respecting property, and in suits between man and man, the parties have a right to a trial by jury; which ought to be held sacred.

XIV. That the people have a right to freedom of speech, and of writing and publishing their sentiments; therefore, the freedom of the press ought not be restrained.

XV. That the people have a right to bear arms for the defence of themselves and the State; and, as standing armies, in the time of peace, are dangerous to liberty, they ought not to be kept up; and that the military should be kept under strict subordination to, and governed by, the civil power.

XVI. That frequent recurrence to fundamental principles, and a firm adherence to justice, moderation, temperance, industry and frugality, are absolutely necessary to preserve the blessings of liberty, and keep government free. The people ought, therefore, to pay particular attention to these points, in the choice of officers and representatives, and have a right to exact a due and constant regard to them, from their legislators and magistrates, in the making and executing such laws as are necessary for the good government of the State.

XVII. That all people have a natural and inherent right to emigrate from one State to another, that will receive them; or to form a new State in vacant countries, or in such countries as they can purchase, whenever they think that thereby they can promote their own happiness.

XVIII. That the people have a right to assemble together, to consult for their common good—to instruct their representatives, and to apply to the legislature for redress of grievances, by address, petition or remonstrance.

XIX. That no person shall be liable to be transported out of this State for trial, for any offence committed within this State.

Chapter II

PLAN OR FRAME OF GOVERNMENT

Section I. The Commonwealth or State of Vermont, shall be governed, hereafter, by a Governor, Deputy Governor, Council, and an Assembly of the Representatives of the Freemen of the same, in manner and form following.

Section II. The supreme legislative power shall be vested in a House of Representatives of the Freemen or Commonwealth or State of *Vermont.*

Section III. The supreme executive power shall be vested in a Governor and Council.

Section IV. Courts of justice shall be established in every county in this State.

Section V. The freemen of this Commonwealth, and their sons, shall be trained and armed for its defence, under such regulations, restrictions and exceptions, as the general assembly shall, by law, direct; preserving always to the people, the right of choosing their colonels of militia, and all commissioned officers under that rank, in such manner, and as often, as by the said laws shall be directed.

Section VI. Every man of the full age of twenty-one years, having resided in this State for the space of one whole year, next before the election of representatives, and who is of a quiet and peaceable behaviour, and will take the following oath (or affirmation) shall be entitled to all the privileges of a freeman of this State.

I ——— ——— *solemnly swear, by the ever living God, (or affirm, in the presence of Almighty God,) that whenever I am called to give, my vote or suffrage, touching any matter that concerns the State of* Vermont, *I will do it so, as in my conscience, I shall judge will most conduce to the best good of the same, as established by the constitution, without fear or favor of any man.*

Section VII. The House of Representatives of the Freemen of this State, shall consist of persons most noted for wisdom and virtue, to be chosen by the freemen of every town in this State, respectively. And no foreigner shall be chosen, unless he has resided in the town for which he shall be elected, one year immediately before said election.

Section VIII. The members of the House of Representatives, shall be chosen annually, by ballot, by the freemen of this State, on the first Tuesday of September, forever, (except this present year) and shall meet on the second Thursday of the succeeding October, and shall be stiled the General Asembly of the Representatives of the Freemen of *Vermont;* and shall have power to choose their Speaker, Secretary of the State, their Clerk, and other necessary officers of the house—sit on their own adjournments—prepare bills and enact them into laws—judge of the elections and qualifications of their own members—they may expel a member, but not a second time for the same cause—They may administer oaths (or affirmations) on examination of witnesses—redress grievances—impeach State criminals—grant charters of incorporation—constitute towns, boroughs, cities and counties, and shall have all other powers necessary for the legislature of a free State; but they shall have no power to add to, alter, abolish, or infringe any part of this constitution. And for this present year, the members of the General Assembly shall be chosen on the first Tuesday of March next, and shall meet at the meeting-house, in *Windsor*, on the second Thursday of March next.*

SECTION IX. A quorum of the house of representatives shall consist of two-thirds of the whole number of members elected; and having met and chosen their speaker, shall, each of them, before they proceed to business, take and subscribe, as well the oath of fidelity and allegiance herein after directed, as the following oath or affirmation, viz.

" I ———— ———— do solemnly swear, by the ever living God, (or, I do solemnly affirm in the presence of Almighty God) that as a member of this assembly, I will not propose or assent to any bill, vote, or resolution, which shall appear to me injurious to the people; nor do or consent to any act or thing whatever, that shall have a tendency to lessen or abridge their rights and privileges, as declared in the Constitution of this State; but will, in all things, conduct myself as a faithful, honest representative and guardian of the people, according to the best of my judgment and abilities."

And each member, before he takes his seat, shall make and subscribe the following declaration, viz.

" I do believe in one God, the Creator and Governor of the universe, the rewarder of the good and punisher of the wicked. And I do acknowledge the scriptures of the old and new testament to be given by divine inspiration, and own and profess the protestant religion."

And no further or other religious test shall ever, hereafter, be required of any civil officer or magistrate in this State.

SECTION X. Delegates to represent this State in Congress shall be chosen, by ballot, by the future General Assembly, at their first meeting, and annually, forever afterward, as long as such representation shall be necessary. Any Delegate may be superceded, at any time, by the General Asembly appointing another in his stead. No man shall sit in Congress longer than two years successively, nor be capable of re election for three years afterwards; and no person who holds any office in the gift of the Congress, shall, thereafter, be elected to represent this State in Congress.

SECTION XI. If any town or towns shall neglect or refuse to elect and send representatives to the General Assembly, two thirds of the members of the towns, that do elect and send representatives, (provided they be a majority of the inhabited towns of the whole State) when met, shall have all the powers of the General Assembly, as fully and amply, as if the whole were present.

---

* The convention which met on July 2, 1777, "ordered that the first election should be holden in December, 1777, and that the General Assembly, thus elected should meet at Bennington, in January, 1778. The publick attention, being arrested by the evacuation of Tyconderoga, and the progress of the enemy under General Burgoyne; the constitution was not printed, seasonable, to have the election holden in December. The convention was therefore, summoned, by the Council of Safety, to meet at Windsor, on the 24th of Dec. 1777." They met and revised the constitution in this particular.

Section XII. The doors of the house in which the representatives of the freemen of this State, shall sit, in General Assembly, shall be and remain open for the admission of all persons, who behave decently, except only, when the welfare of this State may require the doors to be shut.

Section XIII. The votes and proceedings of the General Assembly shall be printed, weekly, during their sitting, with the yeas and nays, on any question, vote or resolution, where one-third of the members require it; (except when the votes are taken by ballot) and when the yeas and nays are so taken, every member shall have a right to insert the reasons of his votes upon the minutes, if he desire it.

Section XIV. To the end that laws, before they are enacted, may be more maturely considered, and the inconveniency of hasty determination as much as possible prevented, all bills of public nature, shall be first laid before the Governor and Council, for their perusal and proposals of amendment, and shall be printed for the consideration of the people, before they are read in General Assembly, for the last time of debate and amendment; except temporary acts, which, after being laid before the Governor and Council, may (in case of sudden necessity) be passed into laws; and no other shall be passed into laws, until the next session of assembly. And for the more perfect satisfaction of the public, the reasons and motives for making such laws, shall be fully and clearly expressed and set forth in their preambles.

Section XV. The style of the laws of this State shall be,—" Be it enacted, and it is hereby enacted, by the Representatives of the Freemen of the State of *Vermont*, in General Assembly met, and by the authority of the same."

Section XVI. In order that the Freemen of this State might enjoy the benefit of election, as equally as may be, each town within this State, that consists, or may consist, of eighty taxable inhabitants, within one septenary or seven years, next after the establishing this constitution, may hold elections therein, and choose each, two representatives; and each other inhabited town in this State may, in like manner, choose each, one representative, to represent them in General Assembly, during the said septenary or seven years; and after that, each inhabited town may, in like manner, hold such election, and choose each, one representative, forever thereafter.

Section XVII. The Supreme Executive Council of this State, shall consist of a Governor, Lieutenant-Governor, and twelve persons, chosen in the following manner, viz. The Freemen of each town, shall, on the day of election for choosing representatives to attend the General Assembly, bring in their votes for Governor, with his name fairly written, to the constable, who shall seal them up, and write on them, votes for the Governor, and deliver them to the representative chosen to attend the General Assembly; and, at the opening of the General Assembly, there shall be a committee appointed out of the Council and Assembly, who, after being duly sworn to the faithful discharge of their trust, shall proceed to receive, sort, and count, the votes for the Governor, and declare the person who has the major part of the votes, to be Governor, for the year ensuing. And if there be no choice made, then the Council and General Assembly, by their joint ballot, shall make choice of a Governor.

The Lieutenant Governor and Treasurer, shall be chosen in the manner above directed; and each freeman shall give in twelve votes for twelve councillors, in the same manner; and the twelve highest in nomination shall serve for the ensuing year as Councillors.[a]

The Council that shall act in the recess of this Convention, shall supply the place of a Council for the next General Assembly, until the new Council be declared chosen. The Council shall meet annually, at the same time and place with the General Assembly; and every member of the Council shall be a Justice of the Peace for the whole State, by virtue of his office.

SECTION XVIII. The Governor, and in his absence, the Lieutenant or Deputy Governor, with the Council—seven of whom shall be a quorum—shall have power to appoint and commissionate all officers, (except those who are appointed by the General Assembly,) agreeable to this frame of government, and the laws that may be made hereafter; and shall supply every vacancy in any office, occasioned by death, resignation, removal or disqualification, until the office can be filled, in the time and manner directed by law or this constitution. They are to correspond with other States, and transact business with officers of government, civil and military; and to prepare such business as may appear to them necessary to lay before the General Assembly. They shall sit as judges to hear and determine on impeachments, taking to their assistance, for advice only, the justices of the supreme court; and shall have power to grant pardons, and remit fines, in all cases whatsoever, except cases of impeachment, and in cases of treason and murder—shall have power to grant reprieves, but not to pardon, until the end of the next session of the Assembly: but there shall be no remission or mitigation of punishment, on impeachments, except by act of legislation. They are also, to take care that the laws be faithfully executed. They are to expedite the execution of such measures as may be resolved upon by General Assembly; and they may draw upon the Treasurer for such sums as may be appropriated by the House: they may also lay embargoes, or prohibit the exportation of any commodity for any time, not exceeding thirty days, in the recess of the House only: they may grant such licenses as shall be directed by law, and shall have power to call together the General Assembly, when necessary, before the day to which they shall stand adjourned. The Governor shall be commander-in-chief of the forces of the State; but shall not command in person, except advised thereto by the Council, and then, only as long as they shall approve thereof. The Governor and Council shall have a Secretary, and keep fair books of their proceedings, wherein any Councillor may enter his dissent, with his reasons to support it.

SECTION XIX. All commissions shall be in the name of the freemen of the State of *Vermont*, sealed with the State seal, signed by the Governor, and in his absence, the Lieutenant Governor, and attested by the Secretary; which seal shall be kept by the Council.

SECTION XX. Every officer of State, whether judicial or executive, shall be liable to be impeached by the General Assembly, either when in office, or after his resignation, or removal for mal-administration. All impeachments shall be before the Governor or Lieutenant Governor and Council, who shall hear and determine the same.

---

[a] The Council of Safety.

SECTION XXI. The supreme court, and the several courts of common pleas of this State shall, besides the powers usually exercised by such courts, have the powers of a court of chancery, so far as relates to perpetuating testimony, obtaining evidence from places not within this State, and the care of persons and estates of those who are *non compotes mentis*, and such other powers as may be found necessary by future General Assemblies, not inconsistent with this constitution.

SECTION XXII. Trials shall be by jury; and it is recommended to the legislature of this State to provide by law, against every corruption or partiality in the choice, and return, or appointment, of juries.

SECTION XXIII. All courts shall be open, and justice shall be impartially administered, without corruption or unnecessary delay; all their officers shall be paid an adequate, but moderate, compensation for their services; and if any officer shall take greater or other fees than the laws allow him, either directly or indirectly, it shall ever after disqualify him from holding any office in this State.

SECTION XXIV. All prosecution shall commence in the name and by the authority of the freemen of the State of *Vermont*, and all indictments shall conclude with these words, "against the peace and dignity of the same." The style of all process hereafter, in this State, shall be,—The State of *Vermont*.

SECTION XXV. The person of a debtor, where there is not a strong presumption of fraud, shall not be continued in prison, after delivering up, *bona fide*, all his estate, real and personal, for the use of his creditors, in such manner as shall be hereafter regulated by law. All prisoners shall be bailable by sufficient securities, unless for capital offences, when the proof is evident or presumption great.

SECTION XXVI. Excessive bail shall not be exacted for bailable offences: and all fines shall be moderate.

SECTION XXVII. That the General Assembly, when legally formed, shall appoint times and places for county elections, and at such times and places, the freemen in each county respectively, shall have the liberty of choosing the judges of inferior court of common pleas, sheriff, justices of the peace, and judges of probates, commissioned by the Governor and Council, during good behavior, removable by the General Assembly upon proof of mal-administration.

SECTION XXVIII. That no person, shall be capable of holding any civil office, in this State, except he has acquired, and maintains a good moral character.

SECTION XXIX. All elections, whether by the people or in General Assembly, shall be by ballot, free and voluntary: and any elector who shall receive any gift or reward for his vote, in meat, drink, monies or otherwise, shall forfeit his right to elect at that time, and suffer such other penalty as future laws shall direct. And any person who shall, directly or indirectly, give, promise, or bestow, any such rewards to be elected, shall, thereby, be rendered incapable to serve for the ensuing year.

SECTION XXX. All fines, license money, fees and forfeitures, shall be paid, according to the direction hereafter to be made by the General Assembly.

SECTION XXXI. All deeds and conveyances of land shall be recorded in the town clerk's office, in their respective towns.

SECTION XXXII. The printing presses shall be free to every person who undertakes to examine the proceedings of the legislature, or any part of government.

SECTION XXXIII. As every freeman, to preserve his independence (if without a sufficient estate) ought to have some profession, calling, trade or farm, whereby he may honestly subsist, there can be no necessity for, nor use in, establishing offices of profit, the usual effects of which are dependence and servility, unbecoming freemen, in the possessors or expectants; faction, contention, corruption and disorder among the people. But if any man is called into public service, to the prejudice of his private affairs, he has a right to a reasonable compensation; and whenever an office, through increase of fees, or otherwise, becomes so profitable as to occasion many to apply for it, the profits ought to be lessened by the legislature.

SECTION XXXIV. The future legislature of this State, shall regulate entails, in such manner as to prevent perpetuities.

SECTION XXXV. To deter more effectually from the commission of crimes, by continued visible punishment of long duration, and to make sanguinary punishments less necessary; houses ought to be provided for punishing, by hard labor, those who shall be convicted of crimes not capital; wherein the criminal shall be employed for the benefit of the public, or for reparation of injuries done to private persons; and all persons, at proper times, shall be admitted to see the prisoners at their labor.

SECTION XXXVI. Every officer, whether judicial, executive or military, in authority under this State, shall take the following oath or affirmation of allegiance, and general oath of office, before he enter on the execution of his office.

THE OATH OR AFFIRMATION OF ALLEGIANCE

" I ——— ——— do solemnly swear by the ever living God, (or affirm in presence of Almighty God,) that I will be true and faithful to the State of *Vermont;* and that I will not, directly or indirectly, do any act or thing, prejudicial or injurious, to the constitution or government thereof, as established by Convention."

THE OATH OR AFFIRMATION OF OFFICE

" I ——— ——— do solemnly swear by the ever living God, (or affirm in presence of Almighty God) that I will faithfully execute the office of ——— for the ——— of ———; and will do equal right and justice to all men, to the best of my judgment and abilities, according to law."

SECTION XXXVII. No public tax, custom or contribution shall be imposed upon, or paid by, the people of this State, except by a law for that purpose; and before any law be made for raising it, the purpose for which any tax is to be raised ought to appear clear to the legislature to be of more service to the community than the money would be, if not collected; which being well observed, taxes can never be burthens.

SECTION XXXVIII. Every foreigner of good character, who comes to settle in this State, having first taken an oath or affirmation of allegiance to the same, may purchase, or by other just means acquire, hold, and transfer, land or other real estate; and after one years residence, shall be deemed a free denizen thereof, and intitled to all the rights of a natural born subject of this State; except that he shall not be capable of being elected a representative, until after two years residence.

SECTION XXXIX. That the inhabitants of this State, shall have liberty to hunt and fowl, in seasonable times, on the lands they hold, and on other lands (not enclosed;) and, in like manner, to fish in all boatable and other waters, not private property, under proper regulations, to be hereafter made and provided by the General Assembly.

SECTION XL. A school or schools shall be established in each town, by the legislature, for the convenient instruction of youth, with such salaries to the masters, paid by each town; making proper use of school lands in each town, thereby to enable them to instruct youth at low prices. One grammar school in each county, and one university in this State, ought to be established by direction of the General Assembly.

SECTION XLI. Laws for the encouragement of virtue and prevention of vice and immorality, shall be made and constantly kept in force; and provision shall be made for their due execution; and all religious societies or bodies of men, that have or may be hereafter united and incorporated, for the advancement of religion and learning, or for other pious and charitable purposes, shall be encouraged and protected in the enjoyment of the privileges, immunities and estates which they, in justice, ought to enjoy, under such regulations, as the General Assembly of this State shall direct.

SECTION XLII. All field and staff officers, and commissioned officers of the army, and all general officers of the militia, shall be chosen by the General Assembly.

SECTION XLIII. The declaration of rights is hereby declared to be a part of the Constitution of this State, and ought never to be violated, on any pretence whatsoever.

SECTION XLIV. In order that the freedom of this Commonwealth may be preserved inviolate, forever, there shall be chosen, by ballot, by the freemen of this State, on the last Wednesday in March, in the year one thousand seven hundred and eighty-five, and on the last Wednesday in March, in every seven years thereafter, thirteen persons, who shall be chosen in the same manner the council is chosen—except they shall not be out of the Council or General Assembly—to be called the Council of Censors; who shall meet together, on the first Wednesday of June next ensuing their election; the majority of whom shall be a quorum in every case, except as to calling a Convention, in which two-thirds of the whole number elected shall agree; and whose duty it shall be to enquire whether the constitution has been preserved inviolate, in every part; and whether the legislative and executive branches of government have performed their duty as guardians of the people; or assumed to themselves, or exercised, other or greater powers, than they are entitled to by the constitution. They are also to enquire whether the public taxes have been justly laid and collected, in all parts of this Commonwealth—in what manner the public monies have been disposed of, and whether the laws have been duly executed. For these purposes they shall have power to send for persons, papers and records; they shall have authority to pass public censures—to order impeachments, and to recommend to the legislature the repealing such laws as appear to them to have been enacted contrary to the principles of the constitution. These powers they shall continue to have, for and during the space of one year from the day of their election, and no longer. The said Council of Censors shall also have power to call a Convention, to meet within two years after their sitting, if there appears to them an absolute necessity of amending any article of this constitution which may be defective—explaining such as may be thought not clearly expressed, and of adding such as are necesssary for the preservation of the rights and happiness of the people; but the articles to be amended, and the amendments proposed, and such articles as are proposed to be added or abolished, shall be promulgated at least six months before the day appointed for the election of such convention, for the previous consideration of the people, that they may have an opportunity of instructing their delegates on the subject.

CONSTITUTION OF VERMONT—1786 * a

WHEREAS all government ought to be instituted and supported for the security and protection of the community as such, and to enable the individuals, who compose it, to enjoy their natural rights, and the other blessings which the Author of existence has bestowed upon man: and whenever those great ends of government are not obtained, the people have a right, by common consent, to change it, and take such measures as to them may appear necessary to promote their safety and happiness.

And whereas the inhabitants of this State have (in consideration of protection only) heretofore acknowledged allegiance to the King of Great-Britain: and the said King has not only withdrawn that protection, but commenced and still continues to carry on, with unabated vengeance, a most cruel and unjust war against them; employing therein not only the troops of Great-Britain, but foreign mercenaries, savages, and slaves, for the avowed purpose of reducing them to a total and abject submission to the despotic domination of the British Parliament, with many more acts of tyranny, (more fully set forth in the Declaration of Congress) whereby all allegiance and fealty to the said King and his Successors are dissolved and at an

---

* Verified from text in "The Constitutions of the Sixteen States which Compose the Confederate Republic of America, according to the latest Amendments, to which are prefixed the Declaration of Independence; the Articles of Confederation; the Definitive Treaty of Peace with Great Britain, and the Constitution of the United States with all the Amendments. Boston: Printed by Manning & Loring, 1797."

"Vermont State Papers; being a Collection of Records and Documents connected with the assumption and establishment of Government by the people of Vermont; together with the Journal of the Council of Safety, the First Constitution, the early Journals of the General Assembly and the Laws from the year 1779 to 1786 inclusive. To which are added the Proceedings of the first and second Councils of Censors. Compiled and published by William Slade, Jun., Secretary of State. Middlebury: J. W. Copeland, Printer, 1823." pp. 567.

a The original constitution of Vermont provided for the election, at intervals of seven years, commencing in 1785, of a "council of censors," who should not only inquire whether the constitution had been preserved inviolate during the last septenary, and whether the government had been faithfully exercised, but should propose such amendments to the constitution as they might deem proper, and call a convention to meet for the adoption or rejection of them. This constitution was adopted by the legislature and declared to be a part of the laws of the State, in March, 1787.

end; and all power and authority derived from him ceased in the American Colonies. And whereas the Territory, which now comprehends the State of Vermont, did antecedently of right belong to the government of New-Hampshire, and the former Governor thereof, viz. his excellency Benning Wentworth, Esq. granted many charters of lands and corporations within this State to the present inhabitants and others. And whereas the late Lieutenant-Governor Colden, of New York, with others, did, in violation, of the tenth command, covet those very lands: and by a false representation, made to the Court of Great-Britain, (in the year 1764, that for the convenience of trade and administration of justice, the inhabitants were desirous of being annexed to that government) obtained jurisdiction of those very identical lands, *ex parte*, which ever was and is disagreeable to the inhabitants. And whereas the Legislature of New-York ever have, and still continue, to disown the good people of this State, in their landed property, which will appear in the complaints hereafter inserted, and in the 36th section of their present Constitution, in which is established the Grants of Land made by that government.

They have refused to make re-grants of our lands to the original Proprietors and Occupants, unless at the exorbitant rate of 2,300 dollars fees for each township; and did enhance the quitrent threefold, and demanded an immediate delivery of the title derived from New-Hampshire.

The Judges of their Supreme Court have made a solemn declaration, that the charters, conveyances, &c., of the lands included in the before-described premises, were utterly null and void, on which said title was founded. In consequence of which declaration, writs of possession have been by them issued, and the Sheriff of the county of Albany sent at the head of six or seven hundred men, to enforce the execution thereof.

They have passed an act, annexing a penalty thereto, of thirty pounds' fine, and six months' imprisonment, on any person who should refuse assisting the Sheriff, after being requested, for the purpose of executing writs of possession.

The Governors Dunmore, Tryon, and Colden, have made re-grants of several tracts of land included in the premises, to certain favourite land jobbers in the government of New-York, in direct violation of his Britannic Majesty's express prohibition, in the year 1767.

They have issued proclamations, wherein they have offered large sums of money for the purpose of apprehending those very persons, who have dared boldly and publickly to appear in defence of their just rights.

They did pass twelve acts of outlawry on the ninth day of March, A. D. 1774, empowering the respective Judges of their Supreme Court to award execution of death against those inhabitants in said district, that they should judge to be offenders, without trial.

They have and still continue an unjust claim to those lands, which greatly retards emigration into any settlement of this State.

They have hired foreign troops, emigrants from Scotland, at two different times, and armed them to drive us out of possession.

They have sent the Savages on our frontiers to distress us.

They have proceeded to erect the counties of Cumberland and Gloucester, and establish courts of justice there, after they were discountenanced by the authority of Great-Britain.

The free Convention of the State of New-York, at Harlem, in the year 1776, unanimously voted, "That all quitrents, formerly due to the King of Great-Britain, are now due, and owing to this Convention, or such future government as shall be hereafter established in this State."

In the several stages of the aforesaid oppressions, we have petitioned his Britannic Majesty in the most humble manner for redress, and have, at very great expense, received several reports in our favour: and in other instances, wherein we have petitioned the late legislative authority of New-York, those petitions have been treated with neglect. And whereas, the local situation of this State from New-York, which, at the extreme part, is upward of four hundred and fifty miles from the seat of that government, renders it extreme difficult to continue under the jurisdiction of said State;

Therefore it is absolutely necessary, for the welfare and safety of the inhabitants of this State, that it should be henceforth a free and independent State, and that a just, permanent, and proper form of government should exist in it, derived from and founded on the authority of the people only, agreeable to the direction of the honourable American Congress.

We the Representatives of the freemen of Vermont, in General Convention met, for the express purpose of forming such a government—confessing the goodness of the great Governor of the universe (who alone knows to what degree of earthly happiness mankind may attain by perfecting the arts of government) in permitting the people of this State, by common consent, and without violence, deliberately to form for themselves such just rules as they shall think best, for governing their future society; and being fully convinced, that it is our indispensable duty to establish such original principles of government as will best promote the general happiness of the people of this State, and their posterity, and provide for future improvements, without partiality for, or prejudice against, any particular class, sect, or denomination of men whatever; do, by virtue of authority vested in us by our constituents, ordain, declare and establish the following Declaration of Rights, and Frame of Government, to be the Constitution of this Commonwealth, and to remain in force therein forever unaltered, except in such articles as shall hereafter on experience be found to require improvement, and which shall, by the same authority of the people, fairly delegated, as this Frame of Government directs, be amended or improved, for the more effectual obtaining and securing the great end and design of all government, herein before mentioned.

Chapter I

A DECLARATION OF THE RIGHTS OF THE INHABITANTS OF THE STATE OF VERMONT

I. THAT all men are born equally free and independent, and have certain natural, inherent and unalienable rights; amongst which are, the enjoying and defending life and liberty—acquiring, possessing and protecting property—and pursuing and obtaining happiness and safety. Therefore, no male person, born in this country, or brought from over sea, ought to be holden by law to serve any person, as a servant, slave, or apprentice, after he arrives to the age of twenty-one years; nor female, in like manner, after she arrives to the age of eighteen years; unless they are bound by their own consent after they arrive to such age; or bound by law for the payment of debts, damages, fines, costs, or the like.

II. That private property ought to be subservient to public uses, when necessity requires it; nevertheless, whenever any particular man's property is taken for the use of the public, the owner ought to receive an equivalent in money.

III. That all men have a natural and unalienable right to worship Almighty God according to the dictates of their own consciences and understandings, as in their opinion shall be regulated by the word of God; and that no man ought, or of right can be compelled to attend any religious worship, or erect or support any place of worship, or maintain any minister, contrary to the dictates of his conscience; nor can any man be justly deprived or abridged of any civil right as a citizen, on account of his religious sentiments, or peculiar mode of religious worship; and that no authority can, or ought to be vested in, or assumed by any power whatsoever, that shall in any case interfere with, or in any manner control the rights of conscience, in the free exercise of religious worship: Nevertheless, every sect or denomination of Christians ought to observe the Sabbath or Lord's day, and keep up some sort of religious worship, which to them shall seem most agreeable to the revealed will of God.

IV. Every person within this Commonwealth ought to find a certain remedy, by having recourse to the laws, for all injuries or wrongs which he may receive in his person, property, or character: he ought to obtain right and justice freely, and without being obliged to purchase it—completely, and without any denial—promptly, and without delay; conformably to the laws.

V. That the people of this State, by their legal representatives, have the sole, exclusive and inherent right of governing and regulating the internal police of the same.

VI. That all power being originally inherent in, and consequently derived from the people; therefore, all officers of government, whether legislative or executive, are their trustees and servants, and at all times, in a legal way, accountable to them.

VII. That government is, or ought to be, instituted for the common benefit, protection and security of the people, nation, or community: and that the community hath an indubitable, unalienable, single man, family, or set of men, who are a part only of that community: and that the community hath an indubitable, unalienable, and indefeasible right, to reform or alter government, in such manner as shall be, by that community, judged to be most conducive to the public weal.

VIII. That those who are employed in the legislative and executive business of the State may be restrained from oppression, the people have a right, by their legal representatives, to enact laws for reducing their public officers to a private station, and for supplying their vacancies in a constitutional manner, by regular elections, at such periods as they may think proper.

IX. That all elections ought to be free and without corruption; and that all freemen, having a sufficient evident common interest with, and attachment to the community, have a right to elect officers, and be elected into office.

X. That every member of society hath a right to be protected in the enjoyment of life, liberty and property; and therefore is bound to contribute his proportion towards the expense of that protection, and yield his personal service, when necessary, or an equivalent thereto: but no part of a man's property can be justly taken from him, or applied to public uses, without his own consent, or that of the representative body of the freemen; nor can any man, who is conscientiously scrupulous of bearing arms, be justly compelled thereto, if he will pay such equivalent; nor the people bound by any law, but such as they have in like manner assented to, for their common good. And previous to any law being made to raise a tax, the purpose, for which it is to be raised ought to appear evident to the Legislature to be of more service to the community, than the money would be if not collected.

XI. That in all prosecutions for criminal offences, a man hath a right to be heard by himself and his counsel—to demand the cause and nature of his accusation—to be confronted with the witnesses—to call for evidence in his favour, and a speedy public trial by an impartial jury of the country, without the unanimous consent of which jury he cannot be found guilty—nor can he be compelled to give evidence against himself—nor can any man be justly deprived of his liberty, except by the laws of the land, or the judgment of his peers.

XII. That the people have a right to hold themselves, their houses, papers and possessions, free from search or seizure: and therefore warrants, without oaths or affirmations first made, affording sufficient foundation for them, and whereby any officer or messenger may be commanded or required to search suspected places, or to seize any person or persons, his, her or their property not particularly described, are contrary to that right, and ought not to be granted.

XIII. That no warrant or writ to attach the person or estate of any freeholder within this State, shall be issued in civil action, without the person or persons, who may request such warrant or attachment, first make oath, or affirm before the authority who may be requested to issue the same, that he or they are in danger of losing his, her, or their debts.

XIV. That when an issue in fact, proper for the cognizance of a jury, is joined in a court of law, the parties have a right to a trial by jury; which ought to be held sacred.

XV. That the people have a right of freedom of speech and of writing and publishing their sentiments, concerning the transactions of government—and therefore the freedom of the press ought not to be restrained.

XVI. The freedom of deliberation, speech, and debate, in the legislature, is so essential to the rights of the people, that it can not be the foundation of any accusation or prosecution, action or complaint, in any other court or place whatsoever.

XVII. The power of suspending laws, or the execution of laws, ought never to be exercised, but by the Legislature, or by authority derived from it, to be exercised in such particular cases only as the Legislature shall expressly provide for.

XVIII. That the people have a right to bear arms, for the defence of themselves and the State: and as standing armies, in the time of peace, are dangerous to liberty, they ought not to be kept up; and that the military should be kept under strict subordination to, and governed by the civil power.

XIX. That no person in this Commonwealth can, in any case, be subject to law-martial or to any penalties or pains, by virtue of that law, except those employed in the army, and the militia in actual service.

XX. That frequent recurrence to fundamental principles, and a firm adherence to justice, moderation, temperance, industry, and frugality, are absolutely necessary to preserve the blessings of liberty, and keep government free; the people ought therefore to pay particular attention to these points, in the choice of officers and represenatives; and have a right, in a legal way, to exact a due and constant regard to them, from their legislators and magistrates, in the making and executing such laws as are necessary for the good government of the State.

XXI. That all people have a natural and inherent right to emigrate from one State to another, that will receive them; or to form a new State in vacant countries, or in such countries as they can purchase, whenever they think that thereby they can promote their own happiness.

XXII. That the people have a right to assemble together, to consult for their common good—to instruct their representatives, and to apply to the Legislature for redress of grievances, by address, petition or remonstrance.

XXIII. That no person shall be liable to be transported out of this State, for trial for any offence committed within the same.

Chap. II

PLAN OR FRAME OF GOVERNMENT

Sect. I. The Commonwealth or State of Vermont, shall be governed hereafter by a Governor, (or Lieutenant-Governor) Council, and an Assembly of the Representatives of the freemen of the same, in manner and form following:

II. The supreme legislative power shall be vested in a House of Representatives of the freemen, or Commonwealth, or State of Vermont.

III. The supreme executive power shall be vested in a Governor, (or, in his absence, a Lieutenant-Governor) and Council.

IV. Courts of justice shall be maintained in every county in this State, and also in new counties when formed; which courts shall be open for the trial of all causes proper for their cognizance, and justice shall be therein impartially administered, without corruption, or unnecessary delay. The Judges of the Supreme Court shall be Justices of the Peace throughout the State; and the several Judges of the County Courts, in their respective counties, by virtue of their offices, except in the trial of such cases as may be appealed to the County Court.

V. A future legislature may, when they shall conceive the same to be expedient and necessary, erect a Court of Chancery, with such powers as are usually exercised by that Court, or as shall appear for the interest of the Commonwealth: Provided they do not constitute themselves the Judges of the said Court.

VI. The legislative, executive and judiciary departments shall be separate and distinct, so that neither exercise the powers properly belonging to the other.

VII. In order that the freemen of this State may enjoy the benefit of election, as equally as may be, each town within this State, that consists or may consist of eighty taxable inhabitants, within one septenary or seven years next after the establishing this Constitution, may hold elections therein, and choose each two representatives; and each other inhabited town in this State may, in like manner, choose each one representative to represent them in General Assembly, during the said septenary or seven years; and after that, each inhabited town may, in like manner, hold such election, and choose each one representative forever thereafter.

VIII. The House of Representatives of the freemen of this State shall consist of persons most noted for wisdom and virtue, to be chosen by ballot by the freemen of every town in this State respectively, on the first Tuesday of September annually forever.

IX. The representatives, so chosen, (a majority of whom shall constitute a quorum for transacting any other business than raising a State tax, for which two thirds of the members elected shall be present) shall meet on the second Thursday of the succeeding October, and shall be styled, *The General Assembly of the State of Vermont:* they shall have power to choose their Speaker, Secretary of the State, their Clerk and other necessary officers of the house—sit on their own adjournments—prepare bills, and enact them into laws—judge of the elections and qualifications of their own members: they may expel members, but not for causes known to their constituents antecedent to their election; they may administer oaths, or affirmations, in matters depending before them—redress grievances—impeach State criminals—grant charters of incorporation—constitute towns, boroughs, cities and counties: they may annually, in their first session after their election, and at other times when vacancies happen, choose Delegates to Congress: and shall also, in conjunction with the Council, annually, (or oftener if need be) elect Judges of the Supreme and several County and Probate Courts, Sheriffs and Justices of the Peace: and also with the Council, may elect Major-Generals and Brigadier-Generals, from time to time, as often as there shall be occasion; and they shall have all other powers necessary for the Legislature of a free and sovereign State: but they shall have no power to add to, alter, abolish, or infringe, any part of this Constitution.

X. The Supreme Executive Council of this State shall consist of a Governor, Lieutenant-Governor, and twelve persons, chosen in the following manner, viz. The freemen of each town shall, on the day of election for choosing representatives to attend the General Assembly, bring in their votes for Governor, with his name fairly written, to the Constable, who shall seal them up, and write on them, *Votes for the Governor*, and deliver them to the representative chosen to attend the General Assembly: and at the opening of the General Assembly, there shall be a committee appointed out of the Council and Assembly, who, after being duly sworn to the faithful discharge of their trust, shall proceed to receive, sort and count the votes for the Governor, and declare the person who has the major part of the votes to be Governor, for the year ensuing. And if there be no choice made, then the Council and General Assembly, by their joint ballot, shall make choice of a Governor.

The Lieutenant-Governor and Treasurer shall be chosen in the manner above directed. And each freeman shall give in twelve votes for twelve counsellors, in the same manner: and the twelve highest in nomination shall serve for the ensuing year as counsellors.

XI. The Governor, and in his absence, the Lieutenant-Governor, with the Council, (a major part of whom, including the Governor or Lieutenant-Governor, shall be a quorum to transact business) shall have power to commissionate all officers—and also to appoint officers, except where provision is or shall be otherwise made by law, or this frame of government; and shall supply every vacancy in any office occasioned by death or otherwise, until the office can be filled in the manner directed by law or this Constitution. They are to correspond with other States—transact business with officers of government, civil and military, and to prepare such business as may appear to them necessary to lay before the General Assembly. They shall sit as Judges to hear and determine on impeachments, taking to their assistance, for advice only, the Judges of the Supreme Court; and shall have power to grant pardons, and remit fines in all cases whatsoever, except in treason and murder, in which they shall have power to grant reprieves but not to pardon, until after the end of the next session of Assembly, and except in cases of impeachment, in which there shall be no remission or mitigation of punishment, but by act of legislation. They are also to take care that the laws be faithfully executed. They are to expedite the execution of such measures as may be resolved upon by the General Assembly: and they may draw upon the Treasurer for such sums as may be appropriated by the House of Representatives. They may also lay embargoes, or prohibit the exportation of any commodity, for any time not exceeding thirty days, in the recess of the House only: they may grant such licenses as shall be directed by law, and shall have power to call together the General Assembly, when necessary, before the day to which they shall stand adjourned. The Governor shall be captain-general and commander-in-chief of the forces of the State, but shall not command in person, except advised thereto by the Council, and then only as long as they shall approve thereof: and the Lieutenant-Governor shall, by virtue of his office, be Lieutenant-General of all the forces of the State. The Governor, or Lieutenant-Governor, and the Council, shall meet at the time and place with the General Assembly: the Lieutenant-Governor shall, during the presence of the commander-in-chief, vote and act as one of the Council; and the Governor, and, in his absence, the Lieutenant-Governor, shall, by virtue of their offices, preside in Council, and have a casting, but no other vote. Every member of the Council shall be a Justice of the Peace for the whole State, by virtue of his office. The Governor and Council shall have a Secretary, and keep fair books of their proceedings, wherein any counsellor may enter his dissent, with his reasons to support it.

XII. The representatives, having met, and chosen their speaker and clerk, shall each of them, before they proceed to business, take and subscribe, as well the oath or affirmation of allegiance herein after directed (except where they shall produce certificates of their having heretofore taken and subscribed the same) as the following oath or affirmation, viz.

You ———— ———— do solemnly swear, (or affirm) that, as a member of this Assembly, you will not propose or assent to any bill, vote, or resolution, which shall appear to you injurious to the people; nor do nor consent to any act or thing whatever, that shall have a tendency to lessen or abridge their rights and privileges as declared by the Constitution of this State; but will, in all things, conduct yourself as a faithful, honest representative and guardian of the people, according to the best of your judgment and abilities. (In case of an oath) So help you God. (And in case of an affirmation) Under the pains and penalties of perjury.

And each member, before he takes his seat, shall make and subscribe the following declaration, viz.

You do believe in one God, the Creator and Governor of the Universe, the rewarder of the good, and punisher of the wicked. And you do acknowledge the scriptures of the Old and New Testament to be given by divine inspiration; and own and profess the Protestant religion.

And no further or other religious test shall ever hereafter be required of any civil officer or magistrate, in this State.

XIII. The doors of the House, in which the General Assembly of this Commonwealth shall sit, shall be open for the admission of all persons who behave decently, except only when the welfare of the State may require them to be shut.

XIV. The votes and proceedings of the General Assembly shall be printed (when one third of the members think it necessary) as soon as conveniently may be, after the end of each session, with the yeas and nays on any question, when required by any member, (except where the votes shall be taken by ballot) in which case every member shall have a right to insert the reasons of his vote upon the minutes.

XV. The style of laws of this State, in future to be passed, shall be, *It is hereby enacted by the General Assembly of the State of Vermont.*

XVI. To the end that laws, before they are enacted, may be more maturely considered, and the inconvenience of hasty determinations as much as possible prevented, all bills which originate in the Assembly shall be laid before the Governor and Council for their revision and concurrence, or proposals of amendment; who shall return the same to the Assembly, with their proposals of amendment (if any) in writing: and if the same are not agreed to by the Assembly, it shall be in the power of the Governor and Council to suspend the passing of such bills until the next session of the Legislature. Provided, that if the Governor and Council shall neglect or refuse to return any such bill to the Assembly with written proposals of amendment, within five days, or before the rising of the Legislature, the same shall become a law.

XVII. No person ought, in any case, or in any time, to be declared guilty of treason or felony by the Legislature.

XVIII. Every man, of the full age of twenty-one years, having resided in this State for the space of one whole year, next before the election of representatives, and is of a quiet and peaceable behaviour, and will take the following oath, (or affirmation) shall be entitled to all the privileges of a freeman of this State.

You solemnly swear, (or affirm) that whenever you give your vote or suffrage, touching any matter that concerns the State of Vermont, you will do it so as in your conscience you shall judge will most conduce to the best good of the same, as established by the Constitution, without fear or favour of any man.

XIX. The inhabitants of this Commonwealth shall be trained and armed for its defence, under such regulations, restrictions, and exceptions, as the General Assembly shall by law direct. The several companies of militia shall, as often as vacancies happen, elect their captains and other inferior officers; and the captains and subalterns shall nominate and recommend the field officers of their respective regiments, who shall appoint their staff-officers.

XX. All commissions shall be in the name of the freemen of the State of Vermont, sealed with the State seal, signed by the Governor, and in his absence the Lieutenant-Governor, and attested by the Secretary; which seal shall be kept by the Council.

XXI. Every officer of State, whether judicial or executive, shall be liable to be impeached by the General Assembly, either when in office, or after his resignation, or removal for mal-administration. All impeachments shall be before the Governor or Lieutenant-Governor, and Council, who shall hear and determine the same, and may award costs.

XXII. As every freeman, to preserve his independence, (if without a sufficient estate) ought to have some profession, calling, trade, or farm, whereby he may honestly subsist, there can be no necessity for, nor use in establishing offices of profit, the usual effects of which are dependence and servility, unbecoming freemen, in the possessors or expectants, faction, contention, corruption and disorder among the people. But if any man is called into public service, to the prejudice of his private affairs, he has a right to a reasonable compensation: and whenever an office, through increase of fees or otherwise, becomes so profitable as to occasion many to apply for it, the profits ought to be lessened by the legislature. And if any officer shall take greater or other fees than the laws allow him, either directly or indirectly, it shall ever after disqualify him from holding any office in this State.

XXIII. No person in this State shall be capable of holding or exercising more than one of the following offices at the same time, viz. Governor, Lieutenant-Governor, Judge of the Supreme Court, Treasurer of the State, member of the Council, member of the General Assembly, Surveyor-General, or Sheriff.

XXIV. The Treasurer of the State shall, before the Governor and Council, give sufficient security to the Secretary of the State, in behalf of the General Assembly; and each High Sheriff, before the first Judge of the County Court, to the Treasurer of their respective counties, previous to their respectively entering upon the execution of their offices, in such manner, and in such sums, as shall be directed by the Legislature.

XXV. The Treasurer's accounts shall be annually audited, and a fair state thereof laid before the General Assembly, at their session in October.

XXVI. Every officer, whether judicial, executive, or military, in authority under this State, before he enter upon the execution of his office, shall take and subscribe the following oath or affirmation of allegiance to this State, (unless he shall produce evidence that he has before taken the same) and also the following oath or affirmation of office, (except such as shall be exempted by the Legislature,) viz.

THE OATH OR AFFIRMATION OF ALLEGIANCE

You do solemnly swear (or affirm) that you will be true and faithful to the State of Vermont; and that you will not, directly nor indirectly, do any act or thing injurious to the Constitution or government thereof, as established by Convention. (If an oath) So help you God. (If an affirmation) Under the pains and penalties of perjury.

THE OATH OR AFFIRMATION OF OFFICE

You ———— ———— do solemnly swear, (or affirm) that you will faithfully execute the office of ———— for the ———— of ————; and will therein do equal right and justice to all men, to the best of your judgment and abilities, according to law. (If an oath) So help you God. (If an affirmation) Under the pains and penalties of perjury.

XXVII. Any delegate to Congress may be superseded at any time, by the General Assembly appointing another in his stead. No man shall be capable of being a delegate to represent this State in Congress for more than three years, in any term of six years;—and no person, who holds any office in the gift of Congress, shall, during the time of his holding such office, be elected to represent this State in Congress.

XXVIII. Trials of issues, proper for the cognizance of a jury, in the Supreme and County Courts, shall be by jury, except where parties otherwise agree: and great care ought to be taken to prevent corruption or partiality in the choice and return, or appointment of juries.

XXIX. All prosecutions shall commence by the authority of the State of Vermont—all indictments shall conclude with these words, *Against the peace and dignity of the State.* And all fines shall be proportionate to the offences.

XXX. The person of a debtor, where there is not strong presumption of fraud, shall not be continued in prison after delivering up and assigning over, *bona fide,* all his estate, real and personal, in possession, reversion, or remainder, for the use of his creditors, in such manner as shall be hereafter regulated by law. And all prisoners, unless in execution, or committed for capital offences, when the proof is evident or presumption great, shall be bailable by sufficient sureties: nor shall excessive bail be exacted for bailable offences.

XXXI. All elections, whether by the people, or in General Assembly, shall be by ballot, free and voluntary: and any elector, who shall receive any gift or reward for his vote, in meat, drink, monies or otherwise, shall forfeit his right to elect at that time, and suffer such other penalty as the laws shall direct: and any person who shall, directly or indirectly, give, promise or bestow any such rewards to be elected, shall thereby be rendered incapable to serve for the ensuing year, and be subject to such further punishment as a future Legislature shall direct.

XXXII. All deeds and conveyances of land shall be recorded in the Town Clerk's office, in their respective towns; and, for want thereof, in the County Clerk's office of the same county.

XXXIII. The Legislature shall regulate entails in such manner as to prevent perpetuities.

XXXIV. To deter more effectually from the commission of crimes, by continued visible punishment, of long duration, and to make sanguinary punishment less necessary, means ought to be provided for punishing by hard labour, those who shall be convicted of crimes not capital, whereby the criminal shall be employed for the benefit of the public, or for reparation of injuries done to private persons: and all persons, at proper times, ought to be permitted to see them at their labour.

XXXV. The estates of such persons as may destroy their own lives, shall not for that offence be forfeited, but descend or ascend in the same manner as if such persons had died in a natural way. Nor shall any article, which shall accidentally occasion the death of any person, be henceforth deemed a deodand, or in anywise forfeited on account of such misfortune.

XXXVI. Every person of good character, who comes to settle in this State, having first taken an oath or affirmation of allegiance to the same, may purchase, or by other just means, acquire, hold and transfer land, or other real estate; and, after one year's residence, shall be deemed a free denizen thereof, and entitled to all the rights of a natural born subject of this State, except that he shall not be capable of being elected Governor, Lieutenant-Governor, Treasurer, Counsellor, or Representative in Assembly, until after two years' residence.

XXXVII. The inhabitants of this State shall have liberty, in seasonable times, to hunt and fowl on the lands they hold, and on other lands not inclosed; and in like manner to fish in all boatable and other waters, not private property, under proper regulations, to be hereafter made and provided by the General Assembly.

XXXVIII. Laws for the encouragement of virtue, and prevention of vice and immorality, ought to be constantly kept in force, and duly executed; and a competent number of schools ought to be maintained in each town for the convenient instruction of youth; and one or more grammar schools be incorporated, and properly supported in each county in this State. And all religious societies, or bodies of men, that may be hereafter united or incorporated, for the advancement of religion and learning, or for other pious and charitable purposes, shall be encouraged and protected in the enjoyment of the privileges, immunities, and estates, which they in justice ought to enjoy, under such regulations as the General Assembly of this State shall direct.

XXXIX. The declaration of the political rights and privileges of the inhabitants of this State, is hereby declared to be a part of the Constitution of this Commonwealth; and ought not to be violated on any pretence whatsoever.

XL. In order that the freedom of this Commonwealth may be preserved inviolate forever, there shall be chosen by ballot, by the freemen of this State, on the last Wednesday in March, in the year one thousand seven hundred and eighty-five, and on the last Wednesday in March in every seven years thereafter, thirteen persons, who shall be chosen in the same manner the Council is chosen, except that they shall not be out of the Council or General Assembly, to be called the Council of Censors; who shall meet together on the first Wednesday of June next ensuing their election, the majority of whom shall be a quorum in every case, except as to calling a convention, in which two-thirds of the whole number elected shall agree; and whose duty it shall be to inquire whether the Constitution has been preserved inviolate in every part, during the last septenary (including the year of their service;) and whether the legislative and executive branches of government have performed their duty, as guardians of the people, or assumed to themselves, or exercised other or greater powers than they are entitled to by the Constitution; they are also to inquire whether the public taxes have been justly laid and collected in all parts of this Commonwealth—in what manner the public monies have been disposed of—and whether the laws have been duly executed. For these purposes, they shall have power to send for persons, papers, and records; they shall have authority to pass public censures—to order impeachments—and to recommend to the Legislature the repealing such laws as appear to them to have been enacted contrary to the principles of the Constitution; these powers they shall continue to have, for, and during the space of one year from the day of their election, and no longer. The said Council of Censors shall also have power to call a Convention, to meet within two years after their sitting, if there appears to them an absolute necessity of amending any article of this Constitution which may be defective—explaining such as may be thought not clearly expressed—and of adding such as are necessary for the preservation of the rights and happiness of the people; but the articles to be amended, and the amendments proposed and such articles as are proposed to be added or abolished, shall be promulgated at least six months before the day appointed for the election of such Convention, for the previous consideration of the people, that they may have an opportunity of instructing their delegates on the subject.

By order of Convention, July 4th, 1786.

MOSES ROBINSON, *President.*

Attest:
  ELIJAH PAINE, *Secretary.*

SELECTED DOCUMENTS

The documents selected for this section have been chosen to reflect the interests or attitudes of the contemporary observer or writer. Documents relating specifically to the constitutional development of Vermont will be found in volume nine of *Sources and Documents of United States Constitutions*, a companion reference collection to the Columbia University volumes previously cited.

SELECTED DOCUMENTS

VERMONT IN 1791

John Lincklaen travelled through Pennsylvania, Vermont and New York in 1791 and 1792. He presents his views of the countryside and the people in this journal.

Source: Travels In the Years 1791 and 1792, Pennsylvania, New York, Vermont. Journals of John Lincklaen. New York and London: G. P. Putnam's Sons, 1893.

JOURNAL.

WE left Albany in the afternoon & slept at New City or Lansingburgh at Platt's Inn, 10 miles from Albany, we went along the North River all the way, passing through a rich well-tilled country inhabited by Hollanders who still preserve their ancient neatness in their houses & their garments, although their language has already become much changed. *Sunday the 25th of September [1791]*

N.B. All the lands on both sides of the river belong to Mr. Van Rensselaer, alias Patroon, for 25 square miles.

From Lansingburgh to Bennington is 30 miles, there are settlements all along the way, lands mediocre, many hills and stony ground. *Monday 26th.*

At Bennington very comfortable at Duis. This place is quite a country town.

The State of Vermont is divided into townships of 6 miles square, divided among 56 proprietors, so that each has something more than 400 acres—which is called a *Grant*. The Legislature never gives more than one to an individual, to prevent undue influence, & to encourage population.

Lands in Bennington township sell at from 15 to 25 D^{lrs} pr. acre. 20 bushels of wheat an acre is considered a good yield.

From Bennington to Shaftesbury 7 miles, all inhabited, from there to Arlington at Merwin's 7 miles—a good public house; from there to Manchester 8 miles at Allis', good tavern, the land good but mountainous & stony, a good harvest is 20 to 25 bushels of wheat an acre. We made the acquaintance of a Mr. Meinders who has a store & a Mr. Smith —these gentlemen told us that lands were selling in this neighbourhood as high as 20 Dolls. the acre.

Tuesday 27th.

Passed through the township of Dorset 5 miles, Harwich 7 miles, Danby 6 miles, where we dined sufficiently well at a Mr. Antony's—this man has sold his farm of 60 acres at 19¼ Dlr. the acre, thence to Wallingford 7 miles to Mrs. Hull's, a good widow's where we were comfortable & found two good beds.

Wednesday 28th.

Passed through Clarendon to Rutland, we stopped on the way at the house of a Thomas Rice, whom we met in the Genesee country, where he had bought 400 acres at 1 Dlr. pr. acre with the intention of settling there. We found there a good farm, land good & well tilled & a new house not even finished. It is astonishing to see a man 50 years

Thursday 29th.

old who has spent the best part of his life in clearing his land & enhancing its value, leaving it all just as he begins to enjoy the fruits of his labor, in order to bury himself anew in the forest, & expose himself to all the difficulties of forming a new settlement! But it is usually the case with Americans, beginning quite poor they buy a few acres in a new country for almost nothing; when after 8 or 10 years of rugged toil they have augmented the worth of their lands, they find themselves with a numerous family, & their little territory, however valuable it may be, does not suffice to support them. Then they sell at a very high price, & so gain a sufficient sum to buy in the Genesee, where the lands are cheaper, three times the quantity, enough to maintain & establish around them a dozen children.

Rutland is quite new, but agreeably situated. we made two good acquaintances, the Sheriff Mr. Sawyer, & Mr. Walker. the former gave me the enumeration of the State of Vermont, which reaches 85,708 souls. Rutland County 15,579. Bennington 12,708. We left there for Pitsford 10 miles.

Left for Middlebury 18 miles, where a Mr. Atley with some others from Canada is building a grain distillery. This establishment will cost them 5,000 Dl^{rs} before it is going. As this country is far from any market they expect to get grain cheap; Hence to Middlebury Falls is 4 miles, there are two roads to Vergennes, we were so unlucky through the stupidity of other people as to take the worst. We found ourselves on the

Friday 30th.

bank of Otter Creek without a Pontoon for crossing. After being detained two hours, we found at last a boat in which we got over, our horses having to swim. Night coming on, we had to pass the night in a poor log house, happily we found kind people there who gave us of their best.

We breakfasted at Vergennes, a new settlement, & pursued a road scarcely practicable to Riches in Charlotte Township where we resolved to stop, Mr. Boon's horse having fallen with him in a hole where he cut himself. _{Saturday, 1 Oct.}

By the laws of Vermont it is not permitted to travel on this day, but we risked being arrested, & started for Burlington Bay, where happily we arrived in the afternoon at Col. Keys. _{Sunday 2nd.} He is obliged to keep tavern by the situation of the place, is truly amiable, has been well educated & has many attainments. We are very comfortable at his house, & very glad to spend some days here to refresh ourselves & recover from the fatigues & the bad roads we have just come through. Burlington is very pleasantly situated on Lake Champlain which there makes a little bay. All the other settlements are new, but people begin to live at their ease. The soil is very rich, particularly for growing wheat & maize, they harvest of the former so much as 40 bushels, but more generally from 20 to 30 bushels the acre, of maize up to 70 bushels, Their greatest traffic is with Canada, they sometimes supply this province with grain, & principally with cattle, & receive in return

European products but the English do not permit the importation of anything manufactured.

When a canal shall have been cut between Skeensborough & the North River, which will be only 6 miles long, & which they have offered to make for 40,000 Livres, all the exports of Vermont will come to New York, but the opinion is that Canada, in order not to lose this branch of commerce, will cut on her side a canal from St. Johns to Chamblee, which will be 12 miles long, but which is easier to build than the other, since use can be made of Little River which flows into the Sorrel River below the rapids; thus Vermont will find herself between two markets & will derive a great advantage from the activity of her neighbours.

The English still retain on Lake Champlain two posts in the territory of the United States. One commanded by a Capt[n] at Pointe du fer in the State of New York, the other on the Island of North Hero in Vermont, where a Serg[t] is stationed with 12 men. There is besides a brig of 16 guns on the Lake.

By the last census the State of Vermont contains 85,708 souls, it is divided into 7 counties, & each county into a number of Townships of 6 miles square. There are no great land holders as in the Southern States. The legislature has always believed it was its policy to grant only a small number of acres to any one person, for the greater preservation of equality, & preventing too great individual influence. This seems to me one reason that the lands have risen to a price so high that they are sold from 10 to 20 Dl[rs] an acre, and it would not even be possible to buy a large quantity at that rate. The largest landowner in the State is a Gen¹ Allen in Chittenden County Colchester Township who has about 120,000 acres. Govr Chittenden 30,000 acres.

There is in the whole State a considerable number of Mapple Trees, but the people do not seem to me to be persuaded of the advantage they might gain from this tree; in the Southern parts where the settlements are older, & the land almost all cleared, the people have cut down almost all the trees, keeping only a small quantity necessary for their own consumption, In the North, where there is more forest, the quantity is more considerable, but no more prized than towards the South. However as these parts are too distant from all markets, people could never raise more grain than they need for their own use, & will consequently be restricted to grazing & cattle, which may lead them to make sugar, since in cutting all trees except the Maple, the pasture is excellent, & much hay can be made, but experience has shown that the ground is so light here, that when the Maples stand alone the least wind uproots them, an inconvenience for which a remedy should be sought. They also say that in these mountains the depth of the snow prevents their gathering sap at the proper time, that towards the South however one man makes 250 lbs. Finally the chief reason for not making sugar is that they have no home market, & that the price of transportation by land is too dear, for the same reason the kettles & other utensils are so hard to get, but to me it does not appear improbable that in forming an establishment in the middle of that part of the State where is the most Maple, that should furnish the inhabitants with the necessary utensils, & that should buy their sugar for ready money, they might be induced to cultivate the trees & gather enough sugar & at a sufficiently reasonable price as to leave a mediocre profit, especially if navigation is opened from Skeensborough to the North River which would greatly lessen transportation charges.

N. B. There are in the State of Vermont, especially to Northward, considerable mines of iron; several forges have already been built at Tinmouth, Wallingford & Fairhaven.

The 3rd, 4th, & 5th.

We waited at Burlington to rest the horses, & ourselves as well from our fatigues. The weather moreover was bad & the blacksmith had no charcoal for shoeing our horses.

Thursday 6th.

We left Burlington at 11 o'clock for Jerico on the Onion River 10 miles, In the afternoon we crossed the river, & went to pay a visit to the Governor of the State, Thomas Chittenden living in the Township of Williston. He received us without ceremony, in the country fashion. He is a man of about 60 years, destitute of all education, but possessing good sense, & a sound judgment, which at once put him at the head of affairs when the States of New York and New Hampshire disputed between themselves the territory of Vermont. It is chiefly to him that the State owes her present Government. He related to us at much length the history of the revolution & how much he had contributed to it, was not ashamed to say that when he placed himself at the head of those who wished a separation from the State of New York, he scarcely knew how to write. Born in the State of Connecticut, he still retains the inquisitive character of his compatriots, & overwhelms one with questions to which one can scarcely reply. He is one of the largest & best farmers of the State, & is believed to own 40,000 acres beside a considerable number of horned cattle. His house & way of living have nothing to distinguish them from those of any private individual but he offers heartily a glass of Grog, potatoes, & bacon to anyone who wishes to come and see him.[1]

We left for Col! Davids in Orange County, township of Montpelier, following the Onion River. This river which runs from East South East to W.N.W. will never be of much consequence for transportation, being interrupted by rapids from time to time. The Road is much better, compared with that along Lake Champlain, but while crossing the chain of the Green Mountains one must continually ascend and descend. *Friday, 7th.*

We left Col! Davids for Judge Paine's in Williamstown 12 miles, road extremely bad, & constantly ascending—on arriving at his house, we found ourselves quite on top of the mountains. He had the kindness to ask us to stay in his log house, which, though made of trees piled one on another, *Saturday, 8th.*

---

[1] See Chipman, *Life of Governor Chittenden.*

has every convenience that can be had in such a dwelling, a thing one rarely finds in these regions, the Americans often contenting themselves with living in the kitchen with their people. His wife is pretty, amiable, & well bred, and made the time pass very agreeably.

NOTES.

Dartmouth Coll.. Pres.^t Wheelock—Woodward—150 students—remaining 4 years for 100 to 150 £ everything included.

Gen'l Enos a frank unceremonious man, had only water to offer us, had travelled everywhere in the U. S.—Conversation about maple trees—sells from 5-8 pence the livre.

Windsor. Legislature. Printer. Dr. Green sends much potash to N. Y. 400 tons this summer.

Waalpoole falls. Mr. Butterfield, acquaintance with Mr. Powldon. Small towns very neat along the Connecticut River, roads mediocre but land well tilled. Superb orchards. a worm eats the fruit.

Springfield (West) Mr. Stebens.

LEGENDS OF SPRINGFIELD

These folktales of the town
of Springfield tell much
about the life and times of
its residents.

Source: Mary Eva Baker. <u>Folklore of Springfield</u>.
Springfield, Vermont, 1922.

Folklore Tales

TO know a few of the quaint and humorous tales of the early home builders of the town may add to our interest and pleasure, and those which are of an amusing character all go to prove the constant vigilance necessary to existence when Springfield was in the making.

In the spring of 1795, Daniel Howe and Elizabeth (Patch) Howe, his wife, came through the woods on an ox sled from Fitzwilliam, N. H., to settle in the new town of Springfield. Their choice of a home was on Monument Hill. By much hard labor they cleared the land and made a large and very productive farm. Here they reared their ten children, whose descendants live in our midst today. They were very prudent, pious people and staunch supporters of the Methodist church.

The writer has often been told by some of the older residents of the town that Mrs. Howe was one of the most remarkable women that ever lived in Springfield. Her fortitude and courage were never daunted. She was a famous spinner and weaver of linen, which she used to sell among the people and at the store, walking from her home to the town and carrying the baby. (Always a baby.) Sometimes she bought a cheese with the sale of her linen. To many of us the problem of transporting a cheese and a baby would require more than ordinary courage. But even this difficulty was quickly overcome by Mrs. Howe; for she carried the cheese some distance along the bridle path, then going back for the baby she would carry the child way past the cheese, and so on until home was reached, with baby and cheese, and in this manner she carried any other purchases she might make.

Again this remarkable woman used to start from her home on horseback with a babe in arms and a bag of corn at the back of the saddle, riding down a bridle path to Goulds Mills.

She forded the river, going up over the hill to the mill in Eureka, where it was ground. Then Mrs. Howe returned the same way, baby and all.

Household utensils were very few and one day her only pail dropped into the well. Unable to get it up, she tied a rope around her waist and demanded to be let down into the well to get the pail. This was done, and she returned in triumph with her treasure.

At an early age she was called as a witness in court. Her father said she was too young to go and testify. He confined her in a hogshead for some time, taking her out at night. Light was admitted by the hogshead's being placed next a window and, while confined there, she embroidered a beautiful apron, the cloth for which she had woven the year before. This is kept as a choice treasure among her descendants in the town today.

Her grandson told of her that she was a "dreadful" worker, and that her husband was "dreadfully" willing she should work.

Mr. Howe, with a neighbor, purchased a dump-cart, each one owning a wheel. Later altercations occurred between them, and as neither one would sell to the other, the children of the two parties took the dump cart and placed it on the boundary line between the two farms. There it stood and went to decay, like "the wonderful one-hoss shay."

When past 75, on a Sabbath day, while all her family were at church and Mrs. Howe was alone, a hawk descended on her chickens. She ran out into the yard, caught up a sledstake, killed the hawk and saved the chickens, receiving a deep wound in one hand. This attracted attention and mention was made of it in the local paper, much to the disgust of "Grandmam Howe," as she was called, and she said, "It was strange a person could not kill a hawk in her own dooryard without the whole town knowing it."

Not all these incidents, or the spinning and weaving of 1200 yards of linen annually, were Mrs. Howe's greatest achievements, but the Christian character she stamped on her children. Her sons and daughters were staunch and true, and her influence, with that of her husband, was felt throughout the town.

Frivolity of all kinds was frowned upon, as she firmly believed life was too serious a thing to waste many precious moments. She and her husband both lived to a great age, as did their children. Grandchildren and great-grandchildren are living in the town today.

Let us carry with us a breath of remembrance of the worthy couple who came in those early days to help in the upbuilding of our town, and to whose memory their grandchildren piled up the rocks on Monument Hill, the highest point on their farm.

* * * * *

No chapter of folklore tales would be complete without reference to Father and Mother Smiley.

With the completion of the meeting house on the Common and the settlement of a minister after so many years of contention and hard feeling, a new era began in the town and the advent of Father Smiley and his talented wife was an occasion of great rejoicing. A large delegation of the people, among them the most prominent in the place, met him at Wentworth's ferry and escorted him with great pomp to his residence, a few rods from the schoolhouse in Eureka.

The party took dinner at Jennison Barnard's, and a reception followed in the evening. There was one Ashabel Draper, who sometimes allowed himself to be overcome by the too free use of ardent spirits, which prevailed on such occasions in those days. The leaders of this affair, wishing to preserve order in the presence of the new minister, gave Draper plainly to understand that his room would be better than his company. Thereupon Draper determined to celebrate the day in his own way and take a sweet revenge upon those whom he considered no better than himself. With the help of a few companions he procured a large potash kettle, inverted it and in some way mounted it like a bell near the route of the procession. Taking a hammer he crawled under it, and as the party went by he tolled the bell as a salute. This kettle is used today as a watering trough near the old Streeter place, now the home of Warren Aldrich.

It was said of Father Smiley, "He was a man of ability; for he could offer a prayer 30 minutes long, and stayed in his pastorate 25 years, which no one has been able to do since." In offering these prayers he always did so with his eyes open. When asked why, Father Smiley replied, "The Bible says, 'Watch and Pray'."

Near the close of his long sermons the men who had toiled early and late during the week would often be drowsy. At such times Parson Smiley, not hesitating to address them personally, would call out, "Mr. Brown" or "Squire Stevens, will you have the goodness to awake!"

Father Smiley was broad in his views. One of his best sermons was on "Worldliness." It came home so closely to one of his hearers that in exasperation he determined to be even with the minister. As he came out of the church he said, "You preached a very excellent sermon today, Mr. Smiley, and I am obliged to you for it, but hadn't you better take a little of it to yourself?" "Oh, most of it, most of it, and what I don't take I hope you will make good use of."

When Father Smiley was a very old man, he would walk up the church aisle tall and straight. His snow white hair was braided in a cue, which was tied with a black ribbon. His face was as white as his hair, and he stood there in the pulpit as though lord of the land. He wore white cotton gloves during the sermon, but they were rarely buttoned and usually half drawn on his hands. His right arm moved slowly back and forth when speaking or praying, and the effect of the flopping fingertips of those white cotton gloves on the light-minded and observing young people may be imagined.

He never spoiled a point for relation's sake. One Sunday morning he preached eloquently on the folly of over-dressing and following after vain fashions when his daughters, as handsomely dressed as any in his church, sat opposite him in the choir. He closed as follows: "You may say, 'It is all very well to preach to others, but why don't you look at home!' My friends I do look at home every day, and my heart bleeds when I do it." If he could not rule his daughters, he did not hesitate to put his parishioners right when he thought they needed it.

Outside the pulpit Mr. Smiley was the real old Irish gentleman, the soul of fun and wit and very fond of his toddy, which was no disgrace then. They tell how a party climbed Ascutney mountain. Arriving at the spring, the parson and Hamlin Whitmore sat down to rest. After the others had gone on, Hamlin drew forth his flask. It was about the time of the first temperance crusade and Mr. Smiley said, "Hamlin, how is this! I thought you had signed the pledge." "So I did, so I did, but you know the clause about its use at the advice of your physician, and I am my own physician." "Hamlin, Hamlin, you rogue, I will let you be my physician today," laughed the parson. The following description of Father Smiley is given us by one who remembers him as he used to come from his home on Cherry Hill. He wore a tall silk hat and a long broadcloth cape reaching nearly to the shoetops. As the wind blew back the folds of the cape, this little girl used to remark, "There comes Father Smiley with his wings spread."

In coming down from his home in Eureka one windy Sabbath morning, as he drew near Captain Lynde's, his tall hat blew off, the wind taking it towards Mt. Ararat, beyond his reach, with his sermons for the day in it. Calling at Mr. Lynde's, he told of his loss and they speedily dispatched a man for the missing hat, who soon brought it back with the sermons unharmed.

Mother Smiley was a quiet woman, not given to much humor or fun. She had a fashion of getting her own way, in the house and out of it. When Father Smiley came into possession of his land and decided to build a new home, Mother Smiley especially wished it to stand true with the compass, and when it was staked out she went home and told her husband it was all wrong. He interviewed the workmen, who maintained that they were right and Mrs. Smiley wrong. Father Smiley reported this to his wife, who said nothing. One very bright moonlight night, when they were living in the old Boutelle home, leaving Father Smiley and all the little Smileys tucked in their beds, she stole out and up the hill and moved the stakes right according to her viewpoint. With wise discretion she remained silent until it was too late to disarrange her civil engineering, and for years after Father Smiley used to delight in telling how once Mother Smiley got the best of him.

One of Mother Smiley's granddaughters writes this:—

"Grandma always sat up late to read by the south window, placing her light on the windowsill. This could be seen from the Common and many homes on the hillside, and the people used to watch for the light in the window; for they knew Mother Smiley was studying—first, her Bible, then history, politics, doings of congress, current events, etc. I do not think there was a woman in Springfield, perhaps not a man, so thoroughly well read as she in those early days. Grandma was never humorous, but more inclined to be serious; was not a great talker, was no gossip, and indulged in very little small talk. She enjoyed discussions on theology with her husband's ministerial friends better than an afternoon spent with her lady friends, hunting up the short-comings of her neighbors. She was a worth-while woman, full of loving charity for all, and ready to help everyone in every way possible."

Father Smiley was chaplain of a regiment which at one time assembled for training in Bellows Falls. At inspection the officer of the day, who was a conceited sort of a fellow, found fault with some detail of the chaplain's uniform and reproved him in words unbecoming an officer and a gentleman. The next public prayer by Chaplain Smiley began as usual, with petitions for the president, the governor, etc., and then—"Oh Lord, bless our inspector, pardon his honest blunders and send down upon him a large measure of wisdom and understanding" rolled out of his mouth in such oily brogue we may be sure the listeners appreciated the point.

The way the parson got his firewood was at least unique. His parishioners gathered one day each winter, when he lived on the farm, and went into the woodlot, felling trees and drawing up the logs to the house. One day's work brought a year's supply of wood. They made half a dozen trips, and the parson had the water over the fire and all the ingredients for a fine glass of hot toddy for the company—at every trip! He passed the toddy himself and, with "I will join you boys," he drank a glass with them. At the close of the day everyone had a very rosy view of life.

In 1825 Father Smiley resigned his pastorate after 24 years of service and spent the remainder of his life here among the people he had loved and served so well.

Mrs. Achsa Emery, for many years a tailoress, whose work brought her into many families in the town, told that she always knew when Parson Smiley arrived where she was working; for after the formal greetings he always inquired: "And how many children have you, madam?"—regardless of how short a time entervened between his calls.

* * * * *

Levi Harlow came to Springfield in 1783, bringing his family on an ox sled. It is said that he made the first brick in town. In 1795 he made brick for Jennison Barnard in Eureka. They mixed the mortar with shovel and hoe.

* * * * *

Elijah Whitney, son of Lemuel, about 1800 was a successful hunter with dog and gun. His sales of peltry were a source of considerable profit in his early life, and he was accustomed to say that he had killed more foxes than Samson turned into the Philistines' corn!

* * * * *

Early Thanksgiving Proclamations

The records of the Vermont Council of Public Safety contain the following item under date of November 14, 1777:—

"Resolved, That Thursday, the 4th day of December next, be and hereby is appointed to be observed as a day of public thanksgiving and prayer throughout the state of Vermont.

"By order of the Council.
JONAS FAY,
Sec'y."

On October 9, 1778, the General Assembly of Vermont voted that Thursday, October 26, be observed as a day of Thanksgiving, and the governor issued, on October 18, a proclamation to that effect, which evidently was the first one ever issued in Vermont. The only copy extant of this proclamation is in the library of Dartmouth college.

The General Lewis Morris chapter, D. A. R., of Springfield has in its possession the original of the following letter of Lewis R. Morris:—

"Gentlemen:

"Inclosed I do myself the honor to transmit you the enclosed Proclamations for a Thanksgiving, that the town of Springfield may have the earliest information of that event. I send two copies that they may be published in the town in such places as they may think proper.

I am Gentlemen
with respect and esteem
your most obedt. servant
L. R. MORRIS,
General Assembly, 1795."

One of the choice treasures of the Vermont Historical society is a chest of rare design, presented by a descendant of Gen. Lewis Morris. This chest was brought to America by the Hessians and was used as a strong box for the money and valuables of the regiment. It was captured at the Battle of Trenton and later fell into the hands of Richard Morris, chief justice of the Supreme court of New York. It was sent by him to his son, Lewis R. Morris, of Springfield, Vt., "to secure your valuables from that dishonest and reckless population of the Green Mountain state, who have held against the just and true claims of New York."

Gen. Lewis Morris was a gentleman educated and accomplished more than was common at that time, of a fine and imposing presence and pleasing manners, a leader in the society of his day. A military training and bearing made him often chosen as commanding officer in the military displays. These circumstances, together with his large property interests, gave him more prominence than perhaps any other man in Springfield or Charlestown enjoyed. His residence on the Connecticut river was for a long time the finest in the country. The location of the mansion fronting the river and meadow, with the rocky Skitchewaug in the background, would be hard to excell in variety and beauty of scenery anywhere. Here he raised a family of stalwart sons and one daughter.

General Morris prided himself on his dining room appointments and service, all meals being served with great dignity. He entertained most lavishly and distinguished guests from all parts of the country came to sit around his board. He dressed with greatest care for each meal and required all members of his family to do the same. Dr. Calvin Hubbard, father of Mrs. Joseph White, was the Morris family physician for many years and, when called professionally, he was expected to wear the best clothes he possessed and remain to the following meal, at which a special topic, previously prepared, was the subject of conversation. A refusal would have been considered very discourteous.

Dr. Hubbard's sister, Ruth, was a tailoress and made all of General Morris' clothes. The finest of broadcloths and the most elegant satins for vests were sent, and Miss Hubbard was expected to cut and fit each and all garments to perfection.

* * * *

The site of the plant of the Fellows Gear Shaper company, which purchased its first parcel of land in 1896, seems to have been the chosen spot for numerous activities in the last one hundred and fifty years. We are told that at first the Indians and wolves held full sway, and until 1836 nothing is written of this particular spot. In that year the Village Falls Manufacturing company, a stock concern, was formed, which owned the woolen mill, cotton mill and other industries. The new company erected on this land a paper mill for making letter paper. The machinery was bought in Claremont, N. H., drawn over Ashley's ferry and thence to Eureka. The road had just been built from the little schoolhouse in Eureka to the ferry. The load was heavy and, when they came to Maple Hill near the Barnard place, they were unable to handle it. Jennison Barnard came to their assistance with five yoke of oxen and drew it up the hill. It being down grade the remainder of the way they met with no further difficulty.

During the business panic of 1837 the Village Falls Manufacturing company failed, and the property came into the hands of Irving Blake, who ran the business until Nathan Wheeler of Grafton, Vt., took it over. At his death, about 1842, Dr. E. A. Knight, who had come to town, married Nathan Wheeler's only daughter and became superintendent of the paper mill, which position he held until 1845. In this year Henry Barnard bought the property and owned it until 1848, when it was destroyed by fire.

Moses Barrett then purchased the lot and erected on it a fully equipped sawmill with all wood-working machinery. He made sash and blinds, doors and other parts for houses.

In 1860 Moses Barrett leased a part of this land to A. J. Fullam for his stencil tool works. This business grew rapidly, and quite a large shop for those times was built. The tools he made cut the letters in a very thin brass sheet in all sizes for marking the largest boxes and also household linen. The receipts from this business reached the *high mark* of $20,000 per year.

There was another rather unusual side to this business. Mr. Fullam was very fond of music and young people, and sang tenor in the Congregational choir. He had a room finished off in one end of the shop, which was handsomely furnished, including a fine piano. Here were held many choir rehearsals and other musical gatherings. Ladies, who were then children, remember numerous sugar parties held here, when tables were spread for the old-fashioned sugar-on-snow. The floor was then cleared and dancing followed. Others remember parties in the summer when they played grace hoops on the lawn and were even served with ice cream, a rare delicacy in those days.

This building was burned about 1867 one very windy night in the early spring. The shingles blew onto Summer street buildings and up onto what is now called Hillcrest, and many men were obliged to climb to the roofs of their houses and pour on water to extinguish fire caused by sparks from these burning shingles.

The next industry here was the Cab Ellis Co-operative Works, where they made fancy wooden boxes, paper boxes, wooden dolls and paper-mache baskets. This venture was not wholly successful and was followed by Slack, Burke & Whitmore, who made fertilizer from old bones and chemicals, which proved very disturbing to the village folks and resulted in its final removal.

From 1886 to 1891 Frank Spellman occupied this location for a paint shop, then J. O. Perkins and W. D. Woolson used it for a time as a dye works.

We will not tell in detail of the various business enterprises in what was known as Cab Shop hollow, or Mineral street; because from Isaac Fisher's small shop for repairing carding machines to the largest shoddy mill in the world is a long story, and we will only mention that there were vats for tanning leather, the making of farm baskets, the first doll cabs ever on the market, a woolen mill and several smaller industries.

* * * * *

Sometime between 1830 and 1837 Jewett Boynton built a cocoonery and hatching shed on what is now known as the Burroughs place in Weathersfield, near Springfield. Mulberry trees were cultivated quite extensively and an attempt was made to establish a profitable business, but the general understanding prevails that as a paying proposition it was a failure. Probably a good many people were familiar with the long shed-like structure which was attached to the residence on the Burroughs farm and which was destroyed by fire only a few years ago. This was the cocoonery and was provided with long tables on which were frames where the silk worms were fed. After they had grown about three inches in length, with plump green bodies, they began spinning the silken thread and winding it round and round themselves, until finally they were entirely enclosed in a cocoon of oval shape. The hatchery was a shed, detached from the other buildings, from which the worms were transferred to the cocoonery. In building these homes for the worms great precaution had to be taken to screen against the squirrels, who considered a few dozen of these, when full grown, a rare delicacy. Some of the mulberry trees are still to be found in the vicinity.

About 1839 an attempt to produce cocoons was made on the farm now owned by Horace Brown, but known to nearly everyone as the Slack farm. The two-story structure, at present forming the main part of the residence, was built for a cocoonery and was situated a little to the east of the site on which it now stands, the present ell being at that time the residence. After about two years' trial, the scheme was abandoned, and the building removed to its present location and converted into the main part of the house.

At nearly the same time Mr. Cady, the father of Mrs.

John A. Slack of Park street, established a cocoonery on Summer Hill at his residence, which was located at the northwest corner of the cemetery, nearly opposite the house now owned by Egbert Davis. His experience was practically the same as already related, and he gave up the idea.

Joseph Messer, who for years lived in the house now occupied by Philip Stern at the foot of the stairs leading from Park to Prospect street, also engaged in the raising of silk worms and one year received the highest bounty from the state for producing the most cocoons. He invented a machine for reeling the silk from these. The silk was then sent to Newport, N. H., where it was twisted, colored and made into a good quality of sewing silk. This was before the seminary was established here, and Mr. Messer one year occupied the old meeting house for feeding and growing his silk worms. The meeting house was on the site of the old high school building, where John Hooper's residence at present stands. The business was not a success because of the climate. The mulberry trees winter killed and the worms sickened and died, and it was finally given up altogether.

Ezekiel Whitcomb had one of the largest cocooneries in this vicinity, on the place where Walter W. Slack now lives. This also was not a success and was destroyed by fire. In the most prosperous year of the industry more than 1000 pounds of cocoons were produced in town.

Raw silk is a continuous thread, and preparation for manufacture includes many distinct operations. The cocoons are first submitted to a treatment that will kill the worm before it begins to force its way out. If the worm eats its way through the walls of a self-constructed prison, the threads will be spoiled; they will be cut into numerous short pieces and will not be good for spinning or twisting.

The methods used are baking the cocoons in an oven heated from 140 degrees to 160 degrees Fahrenheit or by placing them in the hot sun under glass for a few days.

* * * * *

Old deeds are often quaint in their wording and most emphatic and restringent in their demands. The following is a portion of the deed given in the transfer of the Frederick Porter estate, now owned by his daughter, Mrs. Anna Marsh:—

"In front of said house no building is ever to be erected within 4½ rods, beyond the east line of the premises hereby contained, towards the river * * * * no building shall ever be erected in front of said house, nor any obstruction that shall affect the view of the village from the house, but that the land towards the view * * * * in front of said house, shall be forever hereafter occupied solely for cultivation and a passageway to the land adjoining."

There was to be no obstruction between the house now owned by Dr. H. H. Lawrence and the building just above that occupied by the Corliss Hardware company. Strong and binding as this deed runs, not many years lapsed before the opposite side of the street was built up by manufacturing industries.

A Group of Our Oldest Houses

Among the most interesting sights in Springfield now is a group of houses of pioneer days, most of their dates of building clustering around 1800, a time in the history of our town when many obstacles had to be overcome to gather the material for the erection of the then pretentious dwellings. Every citizen in the town today should be justly proud to point these out to the visitor or the passing tourist.

FIRST FRAME HOUSE IN TOWN OF SPRINGFIELD

The oldest of these was built about 1772 by Col. John Barrett, who located on the Connecticut river on what is now the Butterfield farm, known then as the Block House farm. It was the first frame dwelling in town, and the road at that time ran on the other side of the house, between it and the river, with the front door and main entrance on that side.

The Gen. Lewis Morris mansion, also on the Connecticut river a little above the Butterfield place, is perhaps the finest of the group. A tablet was found in the house bearing the date of building, 1795, with the carpenter's name, James Lewis.

According to L. S. Hayes, the interior of the main front part of the house retains the dominant characteristics of the architecture of its period. The original ell has been removed. This contained a large barnlike room that served as a kitchen and living room for the servants, with sleeping accommodations above, and was replaced with the present smaller ell. In the first one there were two eight-foot fireplaces and immense brick ovens. The style of architecture is pure Colonial, a spacious hall extending the width of the house with large rooms on either side and a wide fireplace in each. The lumber used in the construction of the house was cut from the forest nearby and the bricks for the great chimneys were made on the premises. The first shingles on the house were not replaced for a period of 80 years. The mantels, cornices and dadoes are all ornamented with hand carving, done with a penknife. The panels in the wainscotting are made with boards of such width that no joining is visible, and the finish of the interior is of fine selected woods.

Elisha Brown, familiarly known as "Brigadier" Brown, in 1797 built the house now owned by Milton Harlow at the corner of Park and Union streets. In 1802 he built the tavern known as the Holt house, now owned by Myron Whitcomb, in which he took great pride. At his death he left money for its upkeep and his son, Jonathan, ran the tavern until his death and then another son, Enoch, had it for a time. When this tavern was built there were no roads, only bridle paths, marked by blazed trees.

In the old Daniel Field mansion, now the home of Mr. and Mrs. E. C. Beers, we have a house of a type peculiar to itself. It was built in 1799, and its original length was 100 feet, 12 feet having been removed some years since. The fireplaces with their carved mantels and the panelling remain intact today.

The Boutelle house, now owned by J. T. Slack, belongs to this group, as it was built in 1802 by Eliot Lynde. It still retains its original shape.

Father Smiley's house on Cherry Hill was built in 1816, and here again the carved fireplaces have been preserved. We have previously mentioned its early history.

Many anecdotes are told of General Morris, among others the following, told by L. S. Hayes as showing the whole-hearted, generous nature of the man: At one time Mrs. Morris went to Brattleboro with her children for a few days. When General Lewis started to drive down after them, something which he heard in Charlestown changed his plans and he returned home at once. It seems that the kitchen and farm help conceived this to be a proper time for a merry-making and they were preparing a royal dinner, eggs, loaf sugar, raisins and other stores from the parlor larder being freely drawn upon, and all other business stopped. Suddenly the master of the house stood in the kitchen door. Horror seized them, but General Morris, without a frown, went in and, taking the proper utensils, helped prepare the feast, after which he sat down and ate with them, seeing that all were well served of the best. When the meal was ended he said in a tone of confident authority something like this: "Now, boys and girls, you have had a fine frolic and a grand dinner, we have all had a good time, but this won't happen again."

The old house now occupied by Edward Hall and his sisters was built about 1802 or '04. It is of interest to note that the deed given to the grandfather, Caleb Hall, in 1835 was from Leonard Walker, familiarly known as Squire Walker. The wine cellar, 12 feet below the main cellar, is still intact. The barroom was on the south side and fitted up with several little cupboards for storing the wine.

James Litchfield came to Springfield from Scituate, Mass. In 1798 he built the house where Roy Whitney now lives, and the outline is practically the same today. In 1802 he bought land and erected the old Lincoln Ellis house on what was then called "Pine Hill" and there spent the remainder of his days.

In the old D. J. Boynton house at North Springfield we have the distinction of a place where the Indians held their dances. This was built in 1800, and Nathan Lockwood added the brick front in 1819 or '20.

One of Our Pioneer Women

Miss Betsey Barrett, or Aunt Betsey, as she was called by the old and young of two generations, was one of the pioneer women. In her youth she attended school on the Common and the famous school in Eureka, walking every day from her father's house, which he bought in 1791 of Thomas Cook, grandfather of Selden Cook (now the Charles Williams place above the old Lincoln Ellis home), and fitted herself for teaching.

Miss Barrett possessed a strong mind, had the courage of her convictions, and to believe a thing was right was with her to do it. It is related of her that a fire broke out on a Sunday in a building near the river, west of the Falls bridge and the men, not liking to wet their Sunday clothes, were very dainty in handling the water buckets. Aunt Betsey, seeing where the trouble lay, took a bucket and sprang into the mill pond where the water was waist deep and, filling the pail, called on the men to pass the water along.

In those days it was the custom for the taxpayers outside of the village to pay their highway taxes in labor, or "work it out," as it was called. Aunt Betsey, as the owner of a homestead, had a small tax to pay, which she had asked to have abated. This being refused, she declared she would work it out with the men. True to her word, she appeared with her hoe and set the men an example of industry they were not accustomed to. This proved a little too much for them. At noon they told her she could go home and they would work out the remainder of her tax, and it will never be known whether they preferred the additional tax, worked out in their own time, or the quicker pace of Aunt Betsey.

She was very justly proud of her grandfather, Col. John Barrett, one of the pioneers of Springfield. In conversing with others, some incidents in his life she would bring very adroitly in at close intervals.

* * * * *

When the country was new, this region especially was infested with wolves, and it was largely due to Col. Samuel Hunt that it was freed from them at a comparatively early date; for he was a noted hunter of this animal.

The last great public hunt of the kind, it is believed, took place about 1797. A most sagacious wolf had caused no end of disaster, not only in the sheepfolds of Charlestown but also of several other towns in the region. She was too wise to be entrapped, and no marksman was able to approach near enough to shoot her. The people, in desperation at their loss of stock, determined to put an end, not only to her destructive raids, but to her existence. In this the townships of Charlestown, Alstead, Acworth, Langdon, Walpole, Rockingham and Springfield were united. The day was appointed, and Colonel Hunt, who was the leader, laid the trap and all joined him. A circle wide enough to embrace her wolfship was formed at an appointed time, when all approached the center. The men from Springfield were the first to get a glimpse of the wily animal and to start her out. Finding that her territory was too much molested, she did not think best to stop to dispute it but crossed onto the New Hampshire side of the river. This state, affording her no better or safer retreat, the briefest time possible was sufficient to convince her that if there was any safety it must be in return. Again, therefore, she passed over the river, but it was only once more; for the gathering crowd drove her back and forth like a mad creature, vainly attempting to break through the line, when Colonel Hunt rode into the ring and at the first shot from his musket put a terminus both to the hunt and her life. The men were then invited to Colonel Hunt's for refreshment, after which they retired to their homes well satisfied with the day's work.

* * * * *

After Daniel Field had built his log house, about 1780, he returned winters to Rhode Island to work at his trade, that of blacksmith, to pay for his land. During his absence one year in the late fall, Mrs. Field noticed the cattle were being much troubled by some wild animal. She went out to investigate and

WORKSHOP OF DANIEL FIELD, A REVOLUTIONARY
SOLDIER IN WASHINGTON'S ARMY

found a panther stretched along the top rail of the fence. It was of unusual size, and Mrs. Field stated it reached the whole length of the rail. With quick decision she ran into the cabin and snatching a firebrand from the fireplace, she rushed out to fearlessly wave it near the panther, which beat a hasty retreat and did not return.

* * * * *

Mason Walker, whose home was where Will Corliss now lives, used to delight in telling his friends how, when a boy of about 10 years, he went for the cows to the hillside pasture, which was situated between what is now W. D. Woolson's bungalow and the Wiley house. One night it was almost dark when he rounded up the cows to start for home. Suddenly without warning, they took to their heels and left him. Mr. Walker just had time to step into the bushes, when from a nearby thicket emerged a large panther, whose attention was fixed on the retreating cows, and the boy needed no urging to seize the opportunity to climb the nearest tree and await the disappearance of Mr. Panther. In relating this story, Mr. Walker said he never again was caught going for the cows at twilight.

* * * * *

An interesting story is told in connection with the land near the Block house, known as the "heater piece" from its being in the shape of a flatiron. A little later than 1772 one of Col. John Barrett's men forgot to bring his horse from the pasture near the house until after dark. Taking the halter he went out and put it over the head of what he thought was the horse, when a huge black bear reared on its haunches and gave him a sharp cuff, which sent him to the ground, and bruin passed quickly into the nearby woods.

* * * * *

The story is told that when "Brigadier" Elisha Brown had settled on the farm south of C. A. Woolson's present home, a blanket hung in the doorway in lieu of a door, and one night an old bear stuck his head under the blanket.

* * * * *

January 31, 1867, a large panther was killed in the rocky crevices above Downer's hotel. It was believed by some that he came from New York state, while others were just as sure he strayed down along the mountain ranges from Canada. He had been seen by different people for several months before he was finally located among these rocks.

E. Wellman Barnard saw him one time drinking at the spring of the "Big Iron Kettle" (the old iron kettle owned by Dr. Downer and imported from York, England, in 1780). At another time he had attempted to break into Mr. Barnard's sheepfold. He backtracked him from this place to Panther Rock, where he had sought shelter the night before, leaving a portion of his hair frozen to the rock. Mr. Barnard and a companion tracked him through the snow to the place where he was afterwards shot.

* * * * *

These anecdotes furnish sufficient proof of the prevalence of wild animals in this region.

* * * * *

Abner Bisbee, the paternal ancestor of the Springfield branch of the Bisbee family, was one of the first settlers in town. His wife was a resolute and courageous woman, and at one time, while the men were away and when there was an alarm of the approach of Indians, she yoked the oxen and, taking her little ones and other women and children, drove to the Block house, which had been built on the Connecticut river as a place of retreat in time of danger.

* * * * *

In James Whitney's diary is found this rather humorous turkey story: Deacon Lewis, on one occasion while calling at Mr. Whitney's, hitched his horse to the fence, which was fastened to a small tree where the turkeys roosted. The horse, becoming restless, pulled down the fence, which frightened the turkeys and they flew in all directions. Before they could be quieted and persuaded to return to the tree, the foxes secured several of the birds, injuring others so they had to be killed. Deacon Lewis refused to reward Mr. Whitney for the loss. The following night the latter went to Deacon Lewis' house to see what could be done about it. The deacon finally purchased two, weighing four and a half pounds each, at 10 cents per pound, declaring that it was more than the birds were worth to pick their bones.

* * * * *

The following incident was often related by George G. Barnard, son of Jennison Barnard, one of the pioneers of Springfield. Those who remember his pleasant smile and genial manner can imagine him as he told this story which he considered a good joke upon himself: About 100 years ago he used to drive down over the hills from Eureka to call at the home of Deacon Hawkins, where Mrs. Franklin Barney now lives on Summer street. The object of these oft-repeated and prolonged visits was to become better acquainted with the daughter, Mary, who later became his wife. On one of these extended calls Mr. Barnard admitted he stayed later than usual. As he started for home and was just beyond Mt. Ararat, his horse stopped still in the road and refused to go another step. Mr. Barnard, looking about to determine the cause of this abrupt standstill, discovered several peculiar looking objects waving back and forth close by the wall. In telling the story, he admitted his hair "stood on end," and it was some time before he could get up courage to investigate these ghost-like forms. To his surprise he found a flock of geese, disturbed by his late passing, were wagging their heads in mute disapproval. These geese were the property of a colored woman known as "black Lucy," who had a small log house near and by the sale of feathers managed to supply her simple wants. This was her only means of support.

* * * * *

The famous Wells & Newell store on the Hubbard farm in Eureka (now known as the Boothby place) was where the farmers carried their produce to be converted into money to help build the meeting house. Years after when this store was torn down, a secret panel was found in a lower room and, by removing this, all the implements were found for making counterfeit money; also eight dollars in pewter money and as much more of genuine coin. The rats had destroyed most of the script, but a two-dollar bill having the design of an Indian standing upright in a canoe as it passed rapidly down the stream, which to the initiated might imply that this currency must be rapidly passed along, was considered of enough value to be sent to the historical rooms of the Boston Museum, where it has remained until the present time.

* * * * *

The Fletcher seminary, situated in what is now known as Kingdom Valley, just over the line in Chester, deserves more than passing notice.

Daniel Fletcher was born in Chester in 1800. He first taught school in Spencer Hollow. After leaving the neighborhood he became much interested in Christian work and sought to interest his former pupils in the subject of religion. His efforts proved successful and he began to hold meetings in the schoolhouse. He then entered the ministry and married Mary Ann Carley, a governess in Gen. Lewis Morris' family, an educated and accomplished teacher. After retiring from conference work in 1830, he established a young ladies' seminary, to be in charge of Mrs. Fletcher as teacher. It was called Fletcher seminary and had a prosperous existence for six years as to patronage. At one time there were 40 boarding pupils besides some day pupils, the larger portion of them girls. Not proving a financial success, at the end of six years, or about the time the Wesleyan seminary came into existence, it was closed, and the building is now used as a farm house, known today as the Kingdom Valley farm.

* * * * *

If perchance in your rambles for "vantage ground to view the country o'er" you should chance on the top of Sam's Hill, looking to the northwest you will observe the Skitchewaug range, while far away to the northward looms 'Old Ascutney."

With a good glass, looking across the intervening meadows and the winding Connecticut, in the high part of the crest of the former mountain, at a point nearly opposite the old Gen. Lewis Morris place, can be seen a smooth faced overhanging ledge, and at the right an opening. This is the mouth or entrance of the famed and historic "Tory Hole," once a roof aperture or cave several feet in length and breadth, sufficiently roomy to accommodate several persons. From the mouth is a short descent of several hundred feet.

A nearer view can be obtained by passing along the river road, although the way to reach the goal is not from the river side but by a detour either through Spencer Hollow or up through the walnut grove of the old Daniel Gill farm. If you attempt a closer inspection, take along an Alpine staff and cordage and save yourself from the fate of the woman who went a-blueberrying up those rugged sides; and a companion who knows the way may not come amiss.

Before a portion of the roof fell in it was a most blind spot to locate in the pine and hemlock grove about, and you will readily perceive why it might have been a safe retreat for the sympathizers of King George who were not exceedingly popular with their neighbors during and after the period of the Revolutionary war.

If you prefer to tramp it, take the old Crown Point road, visit the oldest burying ground in Springfield on the way, go past the cabin site of Bettergneaw, the first man to hunt beaver along the meadows, and so on to the Hollow road near White's and Wiley's, then along the Weathersfield Bow road to the horse trough, then over a wood road to the walnut grove before mentioned. Passing down the hill and to the right is the wooded crest above the "Tory Hole."

There can be no doubt that the cave was used by both

Indians and whites, as it is well adapted for a place of refuge.

* * * * *

The story of Shem Kemfield and his treacherous career, while familiar to some, seems of sufficient interest to bear repeating.

Previous to 1781 a desperate character and a Tory (Shem Kemfield) lived in town and, because of his many unlawful deeds, was warned to leave and move to Canada. He went, vowing revenge on the inhabitants. In the month of March, 1781, he returned with comrades and took up his abode in the old Tory cave. One morning, the last of the month, the following incident occurred:

He, with three companions, in crossing the Eureka road near the north line of the town was overtaken by Dr. Downer of Weathersfield, returning from Charlestown, N. H., where he had been to see a patient. They made known to the doctor their business, told him they were the vanguard of 50 men who had come to destroy Charlestown and Eureka, and they further told him that it was necessary to take his life to prevent discovery. After much expostulation it was concluded to swear him, Dr. Downer declaring that should they take his life it would be discovered before they could escape. They demanded that he should dismount and kneel before them, crossing himself and vowing to keep the whole affair a profound secret.

Dr. Downer passed on to Lemuel Whitney's and Dr. Cobb's and appeared so singular that they feared for his mental condition. After much hesitation he revealed the whole story to Mr. Whitney and, at the end of some deliberation, the latter sent forth the report that he (Mr. Whitney) had discovered Tories upon the hill east of his house. A messenger was sent down to the river bank opposite Charlestown to signal them. A warning was written on paper, which was attached to a stone and thrown across. A party of armed men soon collected and started pursuit upon the tracks of Kemfield and his band. During the night the inhabitants were everywhere on the alert. The next day three of the invaders were captured on Skitchewaug mountain, near Tory hole, and three others were taken in Charlestown, among them Kemfield, the leader, who was sent to West Point, tried and executed. Before his execution he spent much time trying to figure out who had discovered his plans, but at last he decided that it must have been Dr. Downer, and he longed for an opportunity of revenge.

VERMONT - 1893

The Vermont State Board of Agriculture presed some basic information concerning agriculture, manufactures and the scenery of the state.

Source: Victor I. Spear. *Vermont 1893*. Issued by the State Board of Agriculture, 1893.

AGRICULTURE.

IN few places is it more literally true than in Vermont that agriculture is the foundation upon which all other industries are builded. Until quite recently agriculture has been almost the *only* industry of the State, and very great attention is given to the study of the best methods and the proper lines upon which to work in order to secure the best results. The farming land of Vermont is of great fertility, composed largely of disintegrated rock. It has an enduring quality found in few localities. After a hundred years of cultivation and continuous cropping, it is found, by consulting the census of 1890, that the record of its products takes a high place. In raising wheat only one State produced as much per acre; of corn, two States only exceeded Vermont's record; four States only produced more potatoes to the acre; in buckwheat only one State exceeded Vermont; five States produced more barley per acre; five States produced more rye per acre; one State more oats. Vermont occupies the first place in both quantity and quality of maple sugar produced. Taken as a whole, Vermont takes the first place in a general average of quantity and value of all these farm crops per acre.

From the census it also appears that the average value of farm crops for each person employed is $400, against an average for the United States of $289. It also appears that from 1880 to 1890 the taxable property of the State showed an increase of 86 per cent, the average for the United States being 43.46 per cent. Only sixteen of the States and territories showed as large an increase, and of these all except Florida were west of the Mississippi river, and had received large gains in population. Again, the census shows taxable property to each person in Vermont as $485.98, and an average for the United States of $387.62.

POPULATION.

THE consideration of the foregoing facts naturally leads to an inquiry in regard to the population of the State, and in this it is found that the State has remained nearly stationary. The larger towns have nearly all showed an increase, and the smaller or farming towns have fewer people than ten or twenty years ago. Several causes have contributed to produce this condition, among which may be noted the large emigration that has gone out from the State to settle new territory. The building up of manufacturing and the development of mining and quarrying has tended to draw from the rural districts, and others have not come to fill the places made vacant. This has led to a scarcity of help among the farmers, and the partial or complete neglect in certain localities of good farming land. There has also come a change in the methods of farming, intensive taking the place of extensive methods, and by this means less land is required to produce the same amount than formerly, and this has put a portion of the larger holdings on the market. It is probably true that few localities can offer so good an opportunity to undertake farming on a small capital as Vermont.

The Board of Agriculture has issued a catalogue this season, containing descriptions of about 200 Vermont farms that are at the present time without tenants, and on the market at a very low price. This pamphlet, as well as others issued in recent years by the board, in which Vermont and its industries are described, will be sent to any who may apply for the same to Victor I. Spear, Braintree, Vt.

* * * *

MAPLE SUGAR.

THE single product in which Vermont excels all other States, in both quantity and quality, is maple sugar. The entire product of the country for 1889 was only about 50,000,000 pounds, or less than a pound for each of its population. Of this amount Vermont produced nearly or quite one-third, and in producing it only used from one-third to one-half of the maples of the State. So, although one of the earliest industries of the State, there are few that lack so much of being fully developed as this, and it would seem that a product that is so generally known, appreciated and sought after, should yield a profit sufficient to insure its production to the limit of the capacity of the State.

Improved methods of manufacture, together with an

increasing demand for the best quality as an article of luxury, is doing much to increase production. There is a wide contrast between past and present methods of making maple sugar. In the early days the first settlers used to tap their trees with an axe or tapping iron, catch the sap in troughs dug out of basswood logs, and boil in a kettle swung upon a pole, where it was possible to boil from fifty to one hundred gallons of sap per day, and to make from it a product dark in color, possessing sweetness, and also flavored with the various impurities of charcoal, ashes, leaves, etc., incident to the exposed condition of doing the work. The wooden troughs were first replaced with wooden pails or buckets, and later with tin; the iron potash kettle, first with the small pan, and next the evaporator. The work has been transformed from the open woods to neat and comfortable sugar houses. The sap which used to be carried upon the shoulders of the sugar-makers, making their way much of the time upon snow shoes, is now drawn with teams in suitable tanks or tubs, or conducted through lines of piping direct to the storage provided at the sugar house. All these changes indicate the progress that has taken place in this work, and accounts for the fact that much of the best sugar produced at the present time is suspected of being adulterated, because the *flavor* and *color* of former days is found lacking. At the present time only a few hours after the sap leaves the tree it is in the form of syrup or sugar, and ready to be marketed. The cuts employed show very well past and present methods and conveniences for making maple sugar. Among the best sugar makers sap is seldom, if ever, allowed to stand over night before boiling. Teams or men are kept at work gathering during the day and delivering to the evaporator, which is capable of reducing to syrup with great rapidity, the capacity varying with size of rig from 25 to 100 gallons per hour. By means of this frequent gathering and rapid boiling the sap is in contact with the air but a short time, and discoloring is prevented. Could sap be evaporated without exposure to the air and loss of time, the product would be almost absolutely white.

The market for this product has extended, and the uses for it multiplied. It is little used at present as a domestic necessity, but as a luxury, and large quantities are sold as maple syrup or honey, which is put in air tight packages and sealed while hot, and if properly put up will keep indefinitely.

Maple sugar is used extensively by confectioners for maple candy, by the housewife for making cakes, pies, cookies, etc., it giving a flavor for such uses superior to any other sugar. The demand for the maple product has given rise to much adulteration and counterfeiting, and it is probably true that there is more of the counterfeit than the genuine on the market. To protect their customers against fraud the Vermont maple sugar makers have formed an association, and adopted a trade mark for their goods which is protected by a copyright, and which can only be used under certain restrictions. Persons buying sugar or syrup bearing the label of this association, can be certain of securing a pure and first-class article. The names of the members will be furnished on application to the secretary, A. J. Croft, Enosburgh Falls, Vt.

Though, as has been said, a large part of the available maples are at the present time unused, and though there are farms on the market today for a less price than the value of the maples upon them for sugar purposes, improved methods in making and marketing are having their effect, and the business at the present time is increasing each year.

The early custom of sugar parties, in which whole neighborhoods are invited, has not passed away, and the old and the young gather with old time interest to eat sugar spread upon snow, with the accompaniment of doughnuts; nor has the preference for the scum that rises in process of boiling lost caste. Today the sugar maker tests his syrup by thermometer or hydrometer, knowing exactly the condition of his product, and whether it is fit for syrup, tub sugar or cakes. The custom of testing by means of watching it apron from the ladle or dipper, by dropping in cold water, or blowing from a brown splint, has been superceded by accurate and reliable scientific tests. It is not claimed that all the maple sugar produced in Vermont at the present time is of standard quality; but the proportion of this class of goods is increasing each year, and when so made the industry is found to be profitable. And in proportion as the markets come to know pure from adulterated maple sugar, and the sugar makers learn to produce the best quality of product, will the business increase and become more profitable.

MANUFACTURING.

EXCEPT that, in a certain sense, every home in Vermont did manufacturing in former times, it can be said that very little attention was paid to this business. Artisans in the various trades supplied the demands of the first settlers. The blacksmith, the carpenter, the wheelwright and the cobbler were found in every community pursuing their various vocations. But establishments for producing manufactured goods did not receive early attention. Woolen mills were among the first to be erected to utilize the products of the flocks, but any general efforts in the way of manufacturing are of comparative recent date. There were obstacles in the way of such enterprises, of which the main one was a lack of good roads and cheap transportation facilities. And even when railroads were established, they for a long time failed to appreciate that manufacturing was desirable, and made rates that, as compared with other sections, were practically prohibitory.

More recently, as the State has come to be meshed with railroads, and competition has cheapened transportation from junction points, it has been found profitable to harness a portion of the unlimited water power with which the State abounds, and many important manufacturing plants have grown up and added largely to the material resources of the State. Some of these are closely identified with the State, producing either the products of Vermont genius or Vermont quarries in such proportions as to have commanded the attention of the world, and taken the foremost rank. Of this class is the Fairbanks Scale Works at St. Johnsbury. The Fairbanks scale was the invention of Thaddeus Fairbanks, and the first products were made and produced in a small way, finding a limited sale among his neighbors. Under good management the business grew, until at the present time it occupies buildings as shown in the cut, and claims the largest sale of scales of any factory in the world, and its scales are the standard for all European countries, North and South America, India, China, Japan, Australia, Africa. and the East and West Indies. A close competitor in this department of manufacturing is the Howe Scale Company, located at Rutland. a younger company. that was for a time unfortunate in its management, but at the present is fast winning public favor through the excellence of its workmanship, and gives promise of a successful future.

At Brattleboro is located another industry of Vermont origin, the Estey Organ Works. The Estey organ was the invention of Jacob Estey, and commenced under the most humble circumstances. For several years the inventor used to drive through the country with his own team, selling musical instruments to the people of the adjoining country. Good business tact, together with having produced a good organ, brought its reward, and though since overtaken by flood and other misfortunes, the business has grown to be the largest of its kind in the world, and last year the completion of the last of 250,000 organs was celebrated in a fitting manner. And as in the past, so now, no effort is spared to keep true the claim of the company that the "Estey leads the world."

One of the largest woolen manufactories of New England is located at Winooski, the Burlington Woolen Company. This company uses 5,000 pounds of wool per day, or more than 1,500,000 pounds per year, nearly as much as the State of Vermont produces. Other important woolen mills are located at Hartford, North Hartland, Johnson, Ludlow, Springfield and Bennington, and smaller mills at other places.

The Lane Manufacturing Company, at Montpelier, is the leading firm in New England in producing sawmill machinery. The manufacture of the various wood products are scattered through nearly every town in the State, producing about $4,000,000 worth of goods per annum.

The principal lumber market of the State is Burlington, whose favorable location on Lake Champlain, giving cheap means of transportation to consuming points, has enabled it to maintain its rank as one of the leading markets in the United States.

Besides the works mentioned there are cotton mills, machine shops, foundries, canning factories, shoe factories, paper mills, etc., many of which have lately come into the State, and all of which have found in Vermont conditions favorable to success. Prominent among them is the Vermont Farm Machine Company, of Bellows Falls, which was organized in 1873, and first manufactured an evaporator for maple sap and sorghum. Four years later the manufacture of dairy apparatus was added, and a specialty was made of the Cooley Creamer, which has taken first place among gravity processes of raising cream, and received the gold medal at the Paris Exposition. Over 100,000 of these creamers have been sold. The business of this firm commenced in a room 25 x 30, and has since been enlarged as business has increased, and are now the largest in their line in the United States. The main building of the Company is 365 x 60 feet. They now manufacture a full line of dairy and creamery apparatus, including the Centrifugal Separator, and have a trade extending to all parts of the United States, Europe and Australia.

According to statistics recently taken, it is shown that in the past two years nearly $2,000,000 has been invested in establishing new manufactories in Vermont. This estimate does not include the working capital, but the amount invested in buildings and machinery with which to conduct the business. These various enterprises have utilized many of Vermont's idle water powers, but many others are yet unemployed, and waiting for the person who shall first discover for what purpose they can be profitably turned from their present course and made to perform useful service.

QUARRYING.

CLOSELY allied to, and in many respects a portion of Vermont manufactures is its quarrying, and in treating it under a separate heading it is done because of itself it forms a very important part of Vermont's industrial growth, and because the product in its finished condition represents Vermont's raw material, Vermont labor and Vermont skill. Taken from the mountains, a free gift to those who discover it, there is no expense that enters into this product except the use of capital to conduct the business, and the labor bestowed upon it.

Until very recently this source of wealth has been entirely unknown, and at the present time scarcely a beginning has been made in revealing its possibility, and it requires no strain upon the imagination to foresee greater wealth from beneath the soil in quarrying the various rocks and minerals with which it is underlaid than all that has ever come from the surface. The growth and success of this business to the present time certainly suggest all and more than this.

The marble industry was the first to receive attention, and for a long time was carried on with slight knowledge of the business and with doubtful success. The early means of transportation with teams over poor roads were not such as to favor a business of this kind, and only about half a century ago, it is claimed that so little was known of this business that the entire tract of land now covered by the West Rutland quarries, which was then used for a sheep pasture, was traded even for an old horse of doubtful value. Whether this is true or not it is unnecessary to inquire, as it is known that it might easily have been true of the site of the West Rutland or other quarries of the State at that time. It is only about twenty years since this business took form, and commenced to be conducted in a way to make it profitable. The use of marble has demonstrated its capability of withstanding the effects of air and sun and rain, and no stone is so highly valued for monumental or building purposes. At the present time over half of all the marble used in the United States is quarried in Vermont, and nearly 90 per cent of all monumental marble is obtained here. Quarries of marble are now operated at different points along the western portion of the State, extending from the earliest known black marble of Isle La Motte to the quarries of Bennington county. In 1891 there were 3,317 men employed in this work, receiving in wages and salaries $1,162,746; and capital invested amounting to $7,394,525.

The largest company operating in marble in the world is the Vermont Marble Company, whose headquarters are at Proctor. This company, through its efficient first president, Redfield Proctor, did a great work in simplifying the means of production, and introducing machinery to supplant manual labor in many of the processes of manufacture. It is claimed that the process of sawing marble by means of sand and a toothless strip of iron was the invention of Isaac Markham, of Middlebury.

The claim is made that the entire western part of Vermont is underlaid with a marble formation, of which it is impossible to know anything as to where the valuable deposits are located, except as chance or investigation reveals it. The principal portion of the marble now produced in Vermont is within a radius of five miles from the city of Rutland, and to estimate the future possibilities which may lie in this direction is suggested as a problem suitable to employ the most vivid imagination in its solution.

GRANITE.

YOUNGER than the marble industry, but not less important, is the production of granite. It was quarried as early as 1812, and used for building purposes in walls, window caps, and underpinning to a limited extent, and was found upon the surface throughout a large portion of the State. The building of the second State Capitol of Vermont, nearly sixty years ago, from this material, gave to us one of the finest capitols in New England, and at the same time informed the world of the wealth of this product which lay stored in the granite hills of Barre.

But it is of very recent date that anything has been done toward bringing granite working to the position it now occupies.

In 1875 the town of Barre became connected with the Central Vermont system of railroads by a donation of $55,000 for the building of a branch road. This furnished an outlet for the production of her quarries, and the beginning of the manufacture of monumental work was made. Though still in its infancy, this industry has become of great importance, not only to Barre, but to the State. Another railroad, costing $250,000, has been made to the quarries, and over this road 1,000 tons of granite have been carried in one day, and 100,000 tons, besides 22,000 passengers, in a year. More than 70 acres of quarry have been uncovered, and equipped with the latest improved derricks, steam drills, and other machinery, and the granite works in the village have an aggregate floor space of more than six acres.

If all the plants engaged in the finishing of this material in Barre could be combined in one manufacturing center it would occupy a space of more than 50 acres, give employment to 3,000 men, and pay them yearly

$2,000,000. And this industry is the growth of only twelve years!

The granite business has changed the population of the town from 2,000 to 10,000, increased its valuation from $700,000 to $3,500,000, and furnished monumental work, made from the best quality of granite, to every State in the republic. The manufacturers have an exhibit of Barre granite at the World's Columbian Exposition. It may be seen in the building devoted to manufactures and arts, in the northwest corner.

Their agent at Section H, Group 92, will furnish any information required.

Granite quarries have been opened in other towns, among which are Hardwick, Williamstown, Dummerston, Berlin, Woodbury and Ryegate, and many other localities report large deposits of this mineral, and some are already doing a small business and others organizing. No industry in which Vermont has ever been engaged has employed so large an amount of labor for capital employed as granite, and the production of the State is only limited by the demands of the market.

Slate is another of Vermont's important mineral products, and is a close competitor with marble and granite. It is quarried now principally at Fair Haven and Poultney, in Rutland county. Other localities have quarries that are being worked to some extent, and others that are now idle. Nearly 50 companies are now engaged in this industry, and employed in 1891, 1,323 persons, paying in salaries and wages $572,515 per year. Nearly one-fifth of all the slate produced in the United States comes from Vermont, no State except Pennsylvania producing as much. The improved machinery and methods now employed in this work are likely to render profitable some of the quarries that have been abandoned in the past, and place the business upon a profitable basis, and in this way largely increase the product from the State.

Besides these three leading mineral resources, the State has deposits of others that have been worked to some extent. Among these is copper that has formerly been produced in Vershire and Strafford, employing a large force of workmen. Something is now being done in this work, though the failure of the companies formerly operating, by bad business management, has served to check and retard production. Paint is found at Brandon and has been largely used, is of a durable character, but lacks somewhat in fineness. Iron, talc, soapstone, freestone, asbestos, kaolin, and quartz are also found in several localities, and in some sections something is being done in the way of working them.

SCENERY.

THE scenery of Vermont is a subject that has often engaged the thoughts and pens of the best writers of both this and foreign lands, and each has viewed it from a standpoint of his own, and taken in that portion which was within his range of vision, and each new writer has found a new field and new subjects upon which to exercise his descriptive powers. Its mountains, with their peculiar beauty, timbered and green to their summit, lofty and magnificent in their proportions, and beautiful in their disorderly yet harmonious arrangement, has inspired many an attempt to place them before the world in a word picture as they appeared to the eye. The landscape viewed from the summit of these mountains, in which could be seen villages, farms, lakes, and rivers within a radius of 50 or more miles in either direction, has called forth ardent appreciation, and been often written upon by those who have been privileged to behold it.

The valleys, too, have called forth frequent praise from those who have enjoyed the fine drives along their course. The rivers on their way to the sea, sometimes wild with fury in passing the steep declivities in their course, at other times sluggish while winding their sinuous course through the meadow lands, always clear as crystal and pure as the fountains from which they sprung, have elicited much admiration, both by those who have followed their course in pursuit of the gamey trout with which they abound, and by lovers of nature in either her peaceful or wrathful moods.

The thousands of ponds and lakes hid among the mountains, and surrounded by some of the finest scenery that the eye ever beheld, have afforded pleasant retreats for many a sportsman and lover of nature who annually testify to their appreciation by a return to spend a season in their vicinity. The pure air of the mountains, free from contaminating poisons or germs, which is filled with health and vigor for those who breathe it, has many times been extolled by those whose salvation it has been. The quiet, industrious life of the people, free alike from the enervating influence of wealth or the dependent servility of poverty, and the absence of both aristocracy and peasantry, have elicited much unsought praise from those who have come to know them. The historic interest of Vermont dates back to its first settlement. The Green Mountain Boys at Lake Dunmore, and in their subsequent operations in preparing their attack upon Crown Point and Ticonderoga, the bloody fields of Hubbardton and Bennington, the massacre of Westminster, and the raids of the Indians, have made memorable many localities, and as one comes to know the State, it is a surprise to find how much of its territory is historic because of deeds of heroism or suffering, self-sacrifice or torture that is connected with the spot, and the annals of the State have been well preserved by those who have known of its events.

The love of Vermonters for their State has often been a topic of discussion and sometimes of surprise to those who have known nothing of the conditions, and many things have been written and said in praise of the State as its absent sons have gathered to revive the memories of youth, and to sweeten age with pure draughts of fond recollections of the State of their nativity. Notwithstanding all these things that have been so well written upon or talked about, it is impossible for the stranger to know Vermont until it has been seen. Though hundreds of places and events have been described, there are thousands that neither camera has taken, pencil portrayed, or pen described that are of equal interest and beauty, and events of history and characteristics of the people that are continually new. The feature of Vermont scenery is that its story cannot be told nor pictured. To the lover of nature it is one grand gallery of divine art and beauty, and each step that is taken gives a new point of sight from which the scene puts on a new and different aspect. Perhaps it would be more proper to say that it was beautiful rather than grand, restful instead of exciting, and pleasing rather than surprising. Of all I have seen in the way of description of Vermont scenery, nothing better than the following from the pen of Rev.

William H. Lord has ever come to my attention:

"A rew regions God has made more beautiful than others. His hand has fashioned some dreams or symbols of heaven in certain landscapes of earth; and we have always thought that the Almighty intended, when he formed the hills of Vermont and shook out the green drapery of the forests over their sloping shoulders, and made them fall in folds like the robe of a king along their sides, to give us a dim picture of the new creation and the celestial realm. Italy is a land of rarer sunsets and deeper sky, of haunting songs and grander memories; Switzerland is a region of more towering sublimity and unapproachable grandeur; but in all the galleries of God there is none that so shows the exquisite genius of creative art, the blending of all that is beautiful and attractive with nothing to terrify the eye, the mingling of so much of the material glory, both of the earth and the heavens, with so little to appal the sense. Vermont in summer is the Almighty's noblest gallery of divine art."

Though impossible to even mention the points of peculiar interest in the State, a word of explanation or history is here given of some of the points represented in the engravings we have used. And it is but just to ourselves and to localities that are not given a place to say that the preparation of this work was decided upon just at the approach of winter, and it has been impracticable to take views of scenery to any great extent for this work, and we have been obliged to select and arrange to the best advantage from such material as could be found with our artists.

Lake Dunmore is and will always remain a point of interest to Vermonters, not only from its natural beauty and situation, at the base of the western slope of the Green Mountains, from whose eastern shore there rises to their full altitude the mountain range, with no intervale or cleared or cultivated field to break the rugged character of the scene, but because on its eastern shore was located the earliest rendezvous of the Green Mountain Boys in their organization to resist the authority of New York over land granted by New Hampshire. Also upon the bosom and along the eastern shore are located the scenes of the opening chapters of Thompson's story of the Green Mountain Boys, and according to his narrative the first punishment administered by these mountaineers was a bath to their enemies in the quiet waters of Dunmore.

Farther back in the mountains, and at a short distance from Dunmore, is Silver Lake, one of the clear, beautiful bodies of water in the State, and one which draws many visitors each season.

Of Lake Champlain, of which glimpses of scenery are shown, a proper reference to its many seductive retreats and their magical beauty, or to recall the historic events that have taken place upon its bosom, would fill the entire space at our disposal. It was while sailing up this lake in 1609 that Samuel Champlain first discovered the range of mountains which gave their name to the State. It was upon the waters of this lake that expeditions were fitted out against the colonists during the war of the revolution, and upon this lake at the hands of McDonough that the English received their final chastisement that ever since has remained as a wholesome remembrance. On one of the islands of this lake, La Motte, was erected the first fort upon Vermont soil, and today along the shore and upon the islands of Champlain thousands of people pitch their tents, or come to spend a brief season at some of the hotels, and drink in health, enjoyment and recreation, by partaking of the fruits and products of this beautiful section, and in studying and appreciating its many beauties.

Memphremagog, on our northern boundary, is next in size to Champlain, and has many attractive and striking features. The high and rugged prominence known as Owl's Head, upon its western shore, the islands it contains, the beautiful and thriving village of Newport at its southern extremity, and a rich and thriving farming community upon the east, are a few of the many features that have helped to render this point a favorite resort for many people each season.

Not so well known, but rapidly gaining in prominnence, is Willoughby Lake in the town of Westmore, of which a recent writer has well said: "I believe I am warranted in saying that nature has done more and art less for Willoughby Lake than any other spot in Vermont. Its entire length of six or seven miles, with a breadth of from one to one and a half miles, are so many miles of nature's grandest panorama. High mountains of rugged, bold rock, bound the lake on either side. On the easterly side of the lake is a carriage road, hard, smooth, and near enough to the lake on one side so that the spray from the waves, breaking over the rocks in high wind, does away with the necessity for sprinklers made by hand, while on the easterly side the road is bounded by almost perpendicular mountains, with cooling streams forming cascades equal to those more celebrated in the White Mountains; a lake of clear, cold water, with fish uncaught, enough for many generations." Recently an improvement company has been organized at Willoughby Lake for the purpose of building roads and erecting a large hotel.

At Greensboro is Caspian Lake, located at an altitude of 1,500 feet above the sea, and one of the favorite resorts for camping parties. Several cottages have been erected by those who return year after year to spend their vacation here. The water of this lake is from springs, and always cool and clear. It is a favorite home of the speckled trout, with which it is well supplied. The land adjoining this lake is high and dry, and one of the chief inducements to passing some of one's summer here is in the fact that mosquitoes and malaria are unknown.

Lake Morey, in the town of Fairlee, has also become prominent as a place of resort during the heat of the summer, and the number of people who spend here a portion of each summer is annually increasing. It is not lacking in any of the attractions in the way of natural scenery that go to make Vermont lakes popular as summer resorts, and has an added advantage in being somewhat nearer Boston and the cities of New England than its more northern rivals. Recent investigation as to whom belonged the credit of first applying steam to the propulsion of boats, on the part of the friends of Capt. Samuel Morey, has led to the conclusion that the engine and machinery used by Capt. Morey in his first application of his invention in 1792, was afterwards used to propel a boat upon Lake Morey, and was sunk there between the years 1820 and 1825. Efforts to discover this craft have so far been unavailing, but the point where it was sunk is claimed to be known, and is pointed out with much certainty, and the fact that it has not been found is explained by the muddy character of the bottom of the lake at this place, and the boat is supposed to have sunk into the mud beyond reach, having been filled with stones when it was sunk. Vermonters take quite an interest in the work of Capt. Morey with his first steamboat, especially from the fact that in his last days he was a resident of the State; and it appears reasonably conclusive that fourteen or fifteen years before Fulton made his memorable trip from New York to Albany in 1807, Capt. Samuel Morey steamed up the Connecticut river in a craft of his own construction against the current, at a speed of four miles an hour, and that Fulton afterwards applied the principle of Capt. Morey's craft to the invention for which the world has accorded him credit.

Lake Bomoseen, in Castleton, a body of water containing 15,000 acres, has long been noted as a summer resort, and is well provided with hotel accommodations.

Lake St. Catherine, in Poultney, has also its patrons in seasons of summer travel.

Besides the lakes mentioned the State has some fifteen or twenty others less widely known, having areas of 1,000 to 5,000 acres each, upon whose shores one may find charming sites for summer cottages, and upon whose waters can be found every opportunity to enjoy the pleasures of boating, or rare inducements to indulge in the angler's art.

Of the mountains, of which no attempt will be made either to describe their own intrinsic beauty or the views of surpassing loveliness that may be seen from their summits, probably Mansfield is best known, and accredited with the highest altitude. Fancy has conceived the summit of this mountain in its irregular outline to resemble the appearance of an old man's face turned upward, and the two prominent peaks of the range, designated as nose and chin. suggest that these features are quite prominent in the face represented. Mansfield Mountain is located in Underhill. and has a passable carriage road to the summit.

South of Mansfield, in the town of Duxbury, is seen the summit of Camel's Hump, which is over 4,000 feet above the sea.

Killington, in Sherburne, which is seen from many portions of the State, ranks next to Mansfield in altitude, and has a place in the memory of nearly every one who has been familiar with Vermont.

Like a lone sentinel on guard stands Ascutney on the eastern border of the State. Up from the banks of the Connecticut river, it rises to a height of over 3.300 feet. The pleasant and thriving village of Windsor is at its feet, and large and excellent deposits of granite have been opened upon its side. Unlike most Vermont mountains no trees cover the summit, and no other mountains being near, an unobstructed view can there be obtained for nearly fifty miles in each direction.

Back from the village of Woodstock is Mount Tom, not of high altitude, but of interest, because at great expense the late Frederick Billings built excellent roads to its top and along its sides, which render it attractive and interesting to tourists.

Six miles below Woodstock, along the course of the Ottaquechee river, is found, not a mountain, but a gorge or gulf of considerable notoriety, known as Quechee Gulf. The almost perpendicular sides of this chasm to a depth of nearly 200 feet have served to class it among the points of interest in the State. At the point where the Woodstock railroad crosses this chasm the bridge has a total length of 200 feet, and the distance from the railroad track to the water is 165 feet.

When it is considered that the entire 157 miles from north to south in Vermont is traversed by a high mountain range, it is easily seen how little of this can be referred to. All Vermonters take pride in their mountains, and Sterling and Pico, Jay Peak, Pisgah, and Equinox all have features peculiar to themselves and of interest to the lover of mountain scenery, while rising out of the level country of Addison county, Snake or Grand View Mountain seems higher than many points of greater altitude, and is the pride of the people of the locality, and valued highly for the fine view from its summit.

The economic value of Vermont scenery is a feature new to most of the people of the State, and people who have found their way into the State to spend a portion of each season have, as a rule, come without invitation or inducement from the citizens. Clinging close to the traditions of the past and to former customs, it is but recently that the people of the State have seen any advantage in soliciting a portion of the travel which each season seeks a rest and change by means of a few weeks in some interesting and inviting retreat. The result of the little that has yet been done has been to supply our summer resorts and hotels with more custom than they could accommodate, and many a farmer's home has been utilized to the mutual advantage of both host and guest. New hotels are each year being erected, new sections are being beautified, homes are being opened to this travel, and many are buying small tracts of land and building neat cottages for summer homes for their families, where they may escape the heat, the dust, and disease of the cities, and become strong by close communion with nature, surrounded with her richest privileges.

DOCUMENTS

VERMONT - 1920'S

Wallace Nutting presents some
interesting descriptions of
various Vermont towns and
analyzes city and country life.

Source: Wallace Nutting. *Vermont Beautiful*. Framingham and Boston: Old America Co., Publishers, 1922.

INTERESTING TOWNS

IF we were asked to select an attractive large town of Vermont, we should perhaps name St. Johnsbury. This community, in its edifices, its institutions, and its inhabitants, approaches in some degree toward an ideal. Named by Ethan Allen, developed commercially by the Fairbanks family, a fine type of the Yankee manufacturer of the days before the Civil War, the village of St. Johnsbury gives just the sort of environment to make it a desirable habitation. The broad street, where many dwellings stand back at a dignified distance, is a fine example of comfort without grandeur. While Vermont is too young to possess many good old houses, there is one on this street, the Paddock Mansion, which gives tone to the entire town. It is said that one of the original Fairbanks brothers made its shutters. On page 72, we show from this house a charming parlor, and at the bottom of the same page the quaint woodshed arches and an old " shay " where children play. Dear old " Uncle Sam " Young appears on page 116, taking his leave from this house after a call on Mrs. Taylor, the memory of whose unselfish character is an aroma sweetening still the traditions of the town.

Besides having a notable mansion, St. Johnsbury is dignified by several stone churches, and, through the munificence of the Fairbanks family, by a fine edifice combining library, art gallery, and museum. The old academy is another characteristic feature of this village, being, it is said, the most progressive, most prosperous, best attended, and for college preparatory work, the most successful institution in the state. The railroad and its concomitant evils are kept in a valley below the wide street. Fine elms abound. The maple sugar and syrup industry is largely centered here, and also its product in candies. The scale works stand by themselves on a lower level from the rest of the town so as not to intrude on the residences.

St. Johnsbury is a pleasant center for touring, either into the Vermont hill towns, of which Danbury, lying next, is said to be the most beautiful, or toward Lake Willoughby, a drive unsurpassed, or to the upper Connecticut and the fringes of the White Mountains.

It is gratifying to find, also, in this town a good and leavening number of those citizens who embody the much maligned, but absolutely necessary, New England ideals: a live conscience, an active inquiring mind, and a vigorous acceptance of the work and problems of life as they find it. Perhaps it would not be too much to say that such a town in its ideals and its practical influences means more to America than many other American towns of ten times the population. Views about St. Johnsbury are shown on pages 235, 236, 268, and at the bottom of pages 55 and 244.

Among the resort villages of Vermont, where the market interest is greater than the manufacturing, we may name Woodstock as a typical community. Besides being well supplied with those village institutions which make life attractive within its confines, it has a beautiful situation. It lies in a little empire of its own, near the mountain summits and on the variously appealing Queechee, pages 132, 163, 195, 240. Here was brought to its fullest development the merino sheep, the breeding of which was so marked an enterprise of the last generation. A fine type of breeder, and a deacon of the Congregational church, told me with a laugh in his blue eye of an occasion where he was offered, and declined, for a merino ram a price running into five figures. "It was a case," said he, "of two fools met."

The merino, of longer pedigree than that of most men, excepting those who buy their lineage from delvers in old archives, was doubtless the breed of sheep kept by Abraham. The beautifully convoluted horns, the strongly humped nose, the luxuriant wool, the involuted folds of skin, like the carved linen fold on old chests, the dignified and conceited air of an old merino, are enough to call forth a smile of pleasure from the dullest pessimist and to satisfy the most discriminating artist. On page 27 we show Woodstock sheep, in whose blood is enough of the merino strain to refine the wool without losing the smoother ordinary contours of English sheep.

South Woodstock is a wee village, more a cross-roads, whose abandoned milldam, with its mirror-like surface broken by the stones, made a delightful center before the pole evil became chronic. It was more than a score of years ago that the scene on page 203 stopped our touring, by carriage, for the summer. And it was in and about Woodstock that we first made studies of birches, elms, and pastoral scenes, the last of which, on page 260, called "Feminine Curiosity," had a considerable vogue in its day. The sprightly, deer-like alertness of Jersey cows was caught just as they stopped to inspect us in their path. The fine shady drives of the upper Queechee, with their coppery birches, as on page 31 at the bottom; the old covered bridges at the top of the same page; the birches on page 28; the farm bridge arches on the right of the same page; and the haying scene at the bottom, are all about Woodstock, as are also the pictures of the doorway and the old stagecoach with its wedding party, on page 35.

In Bennington-on-the-Hill we find the best type, perhaps, of the little quiet village, no longer engaged in the world's strenuous activities, yet having a large share of dwellers who have made their mark and are perhaps now crystallizing their experiences.

Windsor claims attention from its age, which, while not hoary, may seem old by comparison with other Vermont towns. Here is Constitution House, an edifice less important architectually than as the birthplace of an independent American republic. As one goes up the hill in Windsor he sees large square houses and a village reminiscent of the better old villages of the Bay State. Windsor has the advantage of contiguity to the fine reaches, north and south, of the Connecticut, and the colony of artists and authors on its shores. Also, Windsor being large enough for good society and near enough to the fine hill country to the west, is a type somewhat like St. Johnsbury, in the character of the men who molded it and in the region that surrounds it.

Continuing our survey of the towns of Vermont, Brattleboro, as the successor of Fort Dummer, the first military outpost of the English in the state, and as the first town of considerable size in the southeast, claims our interest. It was for four years the residence of Rudyard Kipling, whose wife, Caroline Balestier, was born here. The famous "Jungle Books" were begun in Brattleboro. The back country is charming always, but particularly in apple blossom time. On a hill three miles north of the town Kipling built his bungalow, "Naulahka," named for the book written in collaboration with Wolcott Balestier, his wife's brother.

Brandon, many miles northwest of Brattleboro, lies on a plain. It is a place not too large for every man to know his neighbor, and is one of the most beautiful centers in the state. It is prepared to make a visitor's stay there agreeable, either temporarily or permanently. Its roads following Otter Creek are fine, from the number of fascinating view-points they afford. One can approach from Brandon by short and desirable drives the lake region of Dunmore, with its innumerable birches and its reflected mountains. Two roads from Dunmore to the north are available and worth following, besides the roads to Rutland, Bomoseen, and that directly eastward into the mountains.

Manchester is the center of an increasingly fashionable and wealthy set, who have been attracted by the cool airs which draw through its high valley, and by the real magnificence of its mountains. Equinox, page 20, and Dorset Mountain, a little to the north, page 21, are each so fine that they give one more than his share of beauty. The golf links lie circuited by views of these and other peaks.

The stranger in Manchester is startled by the white marble sidewalks, flanked by deep green. Marble is here the most abundant stone. Dorset Mountain, in fact, is composed of marble. Taken in conjunction with the town of Dorset the region about Manchester provides all sorts of aids and comforts for lovers of natural beauty. Dorset village, page 227, is strategically situated for catching all natural delights, as it lies in fair meadows dominated by rounded mountain crests. The Battenkill, which flows through Dorset, is a stream of alluring curves and cool wooded intervals. The clouds above the Battenkill are often glorious. The picture, page 15, taken at Arlington, a few miles below Manchester, gives a vague idea of some of their forms. The sheltered portion of the river is shown on page 16.

In the northern part of Vermont we find such towns as St. Albans, Swanton, on the edge of Quebec, and Essex. As one goes east, with Lake Champlain to the west, no story is needed to call attention to beautiful outlooks. Of course if one wishes to harbor in cities, Burlington in the north, and Rutland in the center of the state, are the points for excursions everywhere.

Burlington has been called the wealthiest, the finest, and the fairest city of its size. The cliff drives near the city afford impressive evidence that one need not go to the sea for wild and bold headlands, for Champlain beats vigorously at times against massive crags, as on pages 76 and 255, whose beetling brows of rock advance as if glorying in the eternal conflict.

In the drives through Rock Park, Burlington possesses a truly remarkable asset of rugged ledges and splendid old forest trees. In the gorge of the Winooski, page 207, near Burlington, we have a fine series of parallel rock walls where the water has used its playthings, the small boulders, to grind away the barriers. In fact those who love to see water at work of its own free will, find in several Vermont streams the action going on whereby huge pot holes are still forming, the stones whirling about in the deep kettles of solid rock, until at last one wall approaches and breaks down another and the gorge is cut deeper. The geologist can find matter of delight here in the Winooski and the picture lover is no less taken up with the fantastic outlines, the seamed walls, the dashing waters, and the changeful color.

Other notable places in Vermont are Middlebury and Northfield, types of those American villages which rejoice in making homes for smaller colleges with the superior advantages of intimate relations impossible in universities. Bellows Falls, in the township of Rockingham, surrounded by a country of rolling contours where hill farms are picturesque to a degree, is itself busy with manufacturing interests. In Rockingham

Center we find an historical old place of worship, the "meeting house," two stories high, with many windows each containing forty lights. West of Bellows Falls is the fair village of Saxtons River with its academy, while to the north lie White River Junction and Hartford, the latter an excellent example of a town of old traditions and well-kept lawns.

It would be superfluous to mention all the little centers of delight in Vermont, and even if this small book were expanded to many volumes one could scarcely stand at all the angles of affection from which the reader has already surmised the author has scanned this state. But at least two towns, Montpelier and Waterbury, may be coupled to illustrate the attractions of the river banks.

Montpelier impresses one as having an extraordinary number of solid edifices in proportion to its size. This may arise partly from the wealth that has been gathered here as the home town of insurance companies; partly because it is the capital of the state; partly owing to the character of its settlers. Montpelier's State House looks out on grounds as good in their way as one could wish. The Winooski is so beautiful, as soon as its waters are freed from the business district, as to be a type of all that is best in a small river. It flows as if designed expressly to elicit our admiration (page 168), and as one follows its north branch there are an equal number of graces which call for a long pause at every turn and every crest of the road. On page 36 is shown a pool with elms. Page 52 gives us another pool, with forest trees and an overflowing cup; also a glimpse of Barre birches; and a curve of the North Branch of the Winooski. We show additional scenes near Montpelier on pages 64, 203, 204, 215, 216, 248 and 291. There is a by-road from Montpelier to Middlesex which is beautiful in summer, but exquisite in autumn. Some of the views of landscape and river just mentioned are found on that road.

The main road passing through Middlesex to Waterbury abounds in interest. The river at Middlesex, as shown at the top of page 80, has cut its way deeply through the rocks and forms here a romantic glen with the mountains framed in the center. It was a rough passage to the bottom of the glen, but it was no small joy to get a standpoint on one of the jagged rocks in the midst of the boiling torrent and answer the wild challenge of its roar.

One can make Waterbury a headquarters for wanderings all the way from Middlesex to Essex. On pages 223, 251 at the bottom, 47, 48, 56 and 64, are some reminiscences of such journeys. The trip to Stowe on the way to Mt. Mansfield, may also come in appropriately from Waterbury. At Stowe we meet as we enter the town a sign: "Go slow, or settle." The period after "settle" is almost as large as the imprint of a man's fist, and was doubtless intended to suggest one. The laconic Vermonter has furnished the tourist a good laugh here, that is, if the tourist is not in a hurry!

On our first journey to Mt. Mansfield to spend a hot Fourth of July we reached the foot only to find a sign on the mountain road, "Automobiles not admitted." That rule has now been abolished, owing to the improvement of the road.

West of Waterbury are beautiful farms, and such cloud effects above the Winooski that painters as yet have failed to transfer them to canvas. At Bolton there are many points of vantage to detain one, the gorge of the Winooski continuing to that town. A swing south to Huntington from the road shows the little tributary stream cutting its tortuous and picturesque course seaward.

One finds much about Ludlow, in passing over the main range, that is worthy of study. On page 176 is a sketch not far west of Ludlow, and at Chester, a winning village, one gets, as on pages 247 and 275, fine specimens of snug farmhouses. Some are set near Swift River, others by little ponds formed by dams. We are sorry to find the word "pond," which was ever in the mouth of the past generation, giving way to "lake." It came to be thought rather countrified to say "pond." But the word is a good one, and ought to be revived. At the bottom of page 44 one sees what roadside birches can do for a farmstead setting. At Cuttingsville, and near it, are remarkably good apple tree settings, as on page 124.

When an old house, possibly abandoned, as on pages 91 and 128, is properly surrounded by apple and lilac bloom, one wishes nothing but to "move in," whatever the condition of the roof. Looking into a cozy homestead, across the water, on page 92, one sees what natural advantages the dweller there has used. Looking out from a cottage door, in the other picture on that page, what could satisfy us more than the picket fence, the corner of the garden, and the wealth of bloom on the old apple tree? How much better than any city dwelling is such a one as this!

CITY AND COUNTRY

WHEN the wrongs of the world are righted it will come about, largely, by perception of what is truly excellent, on the part of the average man. For instance, the family now living precariously in pinched quarters in a city flat will see and know at their worth the hundred thousand unoccupied sites in Vermont, where one may live in the presence of mountains, with the grace of trees; where air and water are free; where the earth is bountiful to the diligent, and where every family may have individuality.

The old English habit of naming a man from his acres, gave him a distinction. He escaped that sameness which marks so many town dwellers, who so far as any individuality is concerned may as well be designated by numbers, like convicts. Are these city dwellers not convicts? Are they not "cabined, cribbed, confined"? Twenty-four hours strike by the tyrants of transportation would bring each of these city dwellers to the immediate danger of starvation. Life is most undignified when it possesses no reserves. Like the multitude of Rome who cried for bread and the circus, our metropolitan populations are fast reaching a condition in which the theatre and the bakery will mark the outward limit of their interests.

It requires, measured in dollars, at least a hundred times as much in town as in country, to secure reasonable immunity from those things which press upon our human nature and deprive it of dignity, power, and poise. Cattle cars are not as subversive of decency to their occupants as are the subways and elevated ways of our cities to their human freight. As a broad principle, whenever men swarm so as to need to live and move in strata, one above another, it is time to get out on God's fair earth. The crowded populations of European slums come to America, and as a rule seek out an American slum as like that they have left as possible. They have been caught by the name America, where the name connotes nothing to them but plenty. They do not know that the plenty is in lands and room. A ghetto is always a ghetto, on whatever continent. And it is always a public shame. When by municipal regulation a room must contain only so many inhabitants, the law does not go deep enough. Intelligently and faithfully enforced the law would give these poor people a chance of life, liberty, and the pursuit of happiness in the country. The gregarious instinct, bred by the experience of countless generations dwelling in hovels under castle walls, as closely as possible, must be bred out from men's constitutions before they can really be men.

The fine specimens of manhood in Europe, bred during the Roman day, in Germany and on the Danube, had the love of country life bred in the bone. An urban population can never be physically fine, unless every family has at least a detached homestead, an idealistic condition never attained in towns exceeding the village size.

There is at present a broadly organized effort to give the children of the poor in cities a little breath of country air, annually. Is this a kindness? It is meant to be. But the act is not based on a wise philosophy. It confesses too much and too little. The propaganda to get children into the country for the summer, if it is a logical movement, rests on the fact that the country is better for the children, But if better for two weeks, why not for four? Why not for fourteen? Why not for fifty-two weeks? The children are needed in the country. They are not needed in the town. They can thrive and grow up to good citizenship in the country, a thing almost impossible in town.

What we need is effort on the part of everybody to get where bread and clothing and shelter and a proper education can be commanded by the efforts of every family for itself. A good education is impossible in town. There is never room enough for the pupils and they must learn exclusively out of books, or dummy models of realities.

The trend of sentiment is toward the establishment of more city parks. But always the park is far from where the poor live. It always will be. The buying up every other block in a city and making it public land would be a burden no city could bear. Americans are often afraid of facts. But the fact is that the street is the playground of the vast majority of city children. Modern conditions make a parent who permits a child to play in the street, a constructive murderer. To confine the child to the festeringly crowded dwelling would make the parent still more a murderer, and there you have it. There is only one answer to the problem. That answer is, the country for the entire year. It is those who are selfish, or ignorant, who huddle in crowded tenements. They love the city because they were bred to it. They are unhappy out of a crowd. A person was telling the author of his cousin, who went from the East Side in New York to visit his relatives in the correspondingly congested district in Boston. Asked how the visit was enjoyed my interlocutor replied, "Oh! he didn't like Boston. Too lonesome." This was equivalent to saying that there was only one spot on earth sufficiently crowded to enable him to feel happy and to feel at home, for the district referred to in New York is supposed to be the most crowded of human habitations!

It is the imperative duty of all governments to see that the people have a chance of life. It is puerile to say that the death rate among city children is less than that in the country. No sane person can suppose that the torrid, airless conditions of the brick hives of a city can be as good for children as the country. If the city is so good for them, why plead for a breath of country air, to save their lives? This reasoning runs in a circle and is based on a narrow generalization. Character, manliness, independence, capacity, a habit of thought, all are encouraged by country life.

Vermont is the nearest rural state to the great cities. It offers something for people of every condition. We remember some years since of a farm of a hundred acres, with comfortable house, good barns and other buildings, a little orchard, a sufficient meadow, pasture, and wood lot, on a good road, only three miles from Woodstock, being offered for five hundred dollars. Conditions have now changed. The value of money has been cut in two, and the value of farms has doubled so that three, perhaps four, times as many dollars might now be required to secure a similar independence. But so far as the capacity of every family in America to secure a dignified independence is concerned, it is being demonstrated every day that the thing is possible, and possible without enduring any conditions to reach the desired estate, which are not far less onerous than are endured every day by the poor in cities.

The funds now expended to take children back to town should be expended in getting their parents settled in the country. No man has a right to live in a city who cannot there secure a fair chance for his children. That is a good American proposition, and tested by it and following on it there would be the greatest exodus in human history.

At present the immigrant, if he intends going onto the land, is often hustled out to the barren side of the prairie states beyond the sufficient rain belt. Dumped on a desert, the immigrant is entirely dependent on the railway to bring him, from long distances, at great prices, timber for a shelter. The consequence is the immigrant digs into the ground and becomes a cave man, living in a sod house, nay, worse than a cave man, for he had solid walls, impregnable against the tempest. The immigrant, who going into the west must be a capitalist, must buy every necessity of human life from a distance. Or if he purchases the fine acres of Iowa or Illinois he will find their price ten times as much as in Vermont. And in the West he will live without that variety which gives life its zest — without hills, without stone for his roads, without the charm and wealth of shade trees or forest.

It has been for long a jest to play upon the hardships of those who live on rocky acres. Men, however, go to Florida and actually blast by dynamite a hole in the stone where they may plant a grapefruit! Is it necessary for any Vermont farmer to blast a hole for an apple tree? Besides, as the finest, and ultimately the only valuable crop is men, Vermont raises more men to the square mile, who count in the energy and the worth of the state, than a whole county in Florida. However well men may start in the tropics or semi-tropics, the second generation is of small account, if they belong to the northern European races.

But is Vermont stony? There are many thousands of acres, in Vermont, without stone enough to build a wall around them. As the hill farms go there is almost always enough land free from stones to make a well balanced farm. The stony part left to pasture and forest is all the better for its stones. An acre of good land, near American villages ruled by American traditions, is worth a township in parts of America better unnamed.

The plain fact is, the finest parts of America for homes, for rearing men have been overlooked in the senseless rush to the West, fostered by paid immigration bureaus. New England, from the farmer's standpoint, or from the outlook of the man who thinks of character and culture, is the least appreciated part of America.

In making the bald statement that a good education can be obtained only in the country, we use the term education in the broadest sense.

The greatest American name of our day, Roosevelt, may be thought to disprove our statement. But the fact that he was born in New York City, when considered in relation to his education, only emphasizes our statement. For the frail child was for long periods taken to the country place on Long Island, and his later years on the plains not only gave him strength, but an insight into practical affairs and a knowledge and love of nature. Thus the greatest figure in recent history was an outdoor man.

If the score of successful city men is tallied, it will appear that great numbers — we believe a good majority — were country bred. Our urban life is either hectic or narrow or debilitating. Only strong men can stand it, and the proportion of those that go under in the nervous strain is large. A constant influx of country life is required. It is common to point to the "unsuccessful" rural citizen. Even from the standpoint of financial success, the country man fails less often than the city man, whose business ventures, as recorded by financial rating, fail nine times out of ten.

New York, or at least the cities, are regarded as the literary centers. But while literary workers sometimes live in towns, we often find they were born in the country. In the eighteenth century there were no cities, in the modern sense. In the nineteenth century, the Cambridge authors, like Lowell and Longfellow, lived on broad, ample grounds, really in the country though in town. Cooper lived in the country. So for the most part did Irving. Bryant's love for the country is well known, and he was not only born in the remote Berkshire hills, but hastened back to them as soon and for as long periods as possible. The great names of Concord also corroborate the truth that country life is loved by literary people.

An education, at least in its primary stages, in the country, gives an understanding of *things*, whereas in the city it gives one mostly a knowledge of books. For many studies, like botany, zoölogy, and geology country life is absolutely required for any proficiency. The overweening conceit of the city man, which appeared up to a recent date in the funny columns and comic illustrations, has changed of late to a better appreciation of the fact that the country man knows how to do more kinds of work than his city brother. A man in town learns to do one thing. The farmer learns to do many. He must be a good merchant, as his success depends entirely upon good buying and selling. Inevitably, if he has any native ability he sharpens his wits by the process of disposing of his produce. The decision as to what he shall plant, what stock he shall keep, and when to dispose of it makes him, at least in these matters, a student of men and things. It is true he may go to bed early, but he has done hours of work before the city man rises, and has this advantage, that he has seen the world at the most beautiful hours of the day.

Politically he has learned much, also. The town meeting, concerning which historians have said so much, is the means of developing political aptitude in the farmer, who understands and follows up the phases of government in the little. It is getting to be known that bad federal government springs out of bad local government. People who conduct their local politics well, are those most worthy to conduct larger affairs.

But there is a primeval, deep-seated reason for the ownership of land. It establishes the possessor as the holder from the Almighty of a section of His earth. The ownership of land has ever been the basis of nobility, as recognized by sovereigns. It is only of late that the distiller and his ilk have been elevated to the peerage. Even now in England the acquirement of a landed estate is the first requisite to give dignity to a title. And when all else has been said, at least everybody depends on the farmer. He holds the situation in his hands, as appears in Russia, where it is found he will not cultivate land if the produce is to be ravished away.

The reader should not infer, however, that the author imagines no good can come out of the city. The city is a necessary evil, and the master mind in banking, trade, and government is compelled to work from the city as a center. But more and more that master mind requires the tonic of country air, and the rugged independence fostered by country life. The Saviour of mankind loved to pass often through the country and consider the lilies. He loved the mountains, the waters, and all growing things; he studied the sky and the sea. Particularly in the last work of his life one notices that he went from Jerusalem every night to the little village of Bethany. One of the finest poems ever written is Lanier's " Into the woods my Master went." It is worthy of being engrossed in the large, to hang on the walls of every farmer's home. It shows very sympathetically the soothing and tender influences of country quiet.

We would like to leave this aspect of our subject with the reflection that God made the country and enjoys it Himself, and that any proper religion suggests a study of and a joy in what is made beautiful for us. All our thoughts should be shot through with reverence at the view of a sunset. We cannot refrain from narrating a recent experience. Returning one day from town we saw in the west a thousand mottled clouds. They began to extend north and south and to rise toward the zenith. Their color was delicate rather than gaudy. They rose steadily, symmetrically, until they covered a third of the heavens. Simultaneously my companion and I exclaimed: " An Archangel's wings! " It was all so noble to see, so soothing, so inspiring. Certainly life seems finer in the country whether it is so or not. Scarcely has there been a time when it has not appealed to the poets, from that unnamed one who told of man in his first garden, to the latest contributor in the local paper.

The day's work is over. The waving grain grows still. The hills take on a darker purple. The sky grows nearer. The call of the whippoor-will comes from the woodland to the leeward. A delicate soft air envelops all. An apple, well ripened, falls in the home orchard. The flash of a swallow noiselessly sweeps past in the early gloaming. The world is seeking to forget strife and to listen reverently. "When twilight lets her curtain down and pins it with a star," we see in the country a perfect world.

THE BEAUTY OF A CORNFIELD

VERMONT has an admirable soil for corn, and no finer feature of its summer landscape could appeal to us than a cornfield, well kept. As soon as its waving blades cover the ground in the latter part of July, the successive beauties of the corn begin to entrance us. The pollen stalk raises its multiple cross and sheds its golden dust; the silken tassel hangs daintily from the ear tip; the luscious green envelope, leaf after leaf, folds in the sweet grains. As the season advances, and we see corn in the shock, with the golden squash or pumpkins between the rows, there is a new appeal, a changed beauty. England without this glory of growing corn, lacks much in inspiration for her poets and painters. We await in America those who no doubt will sing with finer rapture than their predecessors the joy of the cornfield.

No food, in a growing state, could be more fraught with beauty, poetry, and the sense of plenty than the corn. The hearts of the Pilgrim Fathers were lightened when first they heard the rustling corn and sensed their relief from want. From the time when the bobolink, bubbling over with full-throated melody, accompanies the farmer's boy in the planting of the corn, to the gathering in, on the great barn floor, of the mellow harvest, the corn supplies us with a sequence of imaginative suggestions. In every stage and aspect it is a delight. A stroll among its tall rows soothes our nerves better than the poppy, and seeing it in generous autumn we have a striking symbol of natural wealth and of the joyous response of the earth to her children. Its long braids of seed ears, hanging on the gable of the barn, as on page 283, are at once a decoration and a prophecy.

Why have not painters used more often the motive of a cluster of corn ears? In both their ripened and their green state they are beautiful. The occasional glimpse of white kernels, where the green husk has partially uncovered them, is not surpassed by anything in nature.

Students of corn say that it has been brought to its present state from a diminutive nubbin ear. However that may be, we know that it responds when we help it in an effort to reach an ideal perfection. By the selection of the plump grains, and by discarding the undeveloped tip grains, much has been done to improve the fullness and weight of the corn ear. Furthermore, by recent adoption of green corn silage the growing of corn has been much increased. As America's indigenous contribution to the world's food store, corn has a patriotic appeal and should be a state symbol.

DOCUMENTS

BASIC FACTS

Capital City .... Montpelier
Nickname .... The Green Mountain State
Flower .... Red Clover
Bird .... Hermit Thrush
Tree .... Sugar Maple
Song .... *Hail, Vermont!*
Animal .... Morgan Horse
Entered the Union .... March 4, 1791

STATISTICS*

Land Area (square miles) 9,267
    Rank in Nation 43rd
Population† 460,000
    Rank in Nation 48th
    Density per square mile 49.6
Number of Representatives in Congress 1
Capital City .... Montpelier
    Population 8,609
    Rank in State 10th
Largest City .... Burlington
    Population 38,633
Number of Cities and Towns over
    10,000 Population‡ 8
Number of Counties 14

---

* Based on 1970 census statistics compiled by the Bureau of the Census.
† Estimated by Bureau of the Census for July 1, 1972.
‡ Includes 5 towns over 10,000 population.

VERMONT

MAP OF CONGRESSIONAL DISTRICTS
OF VERMONT

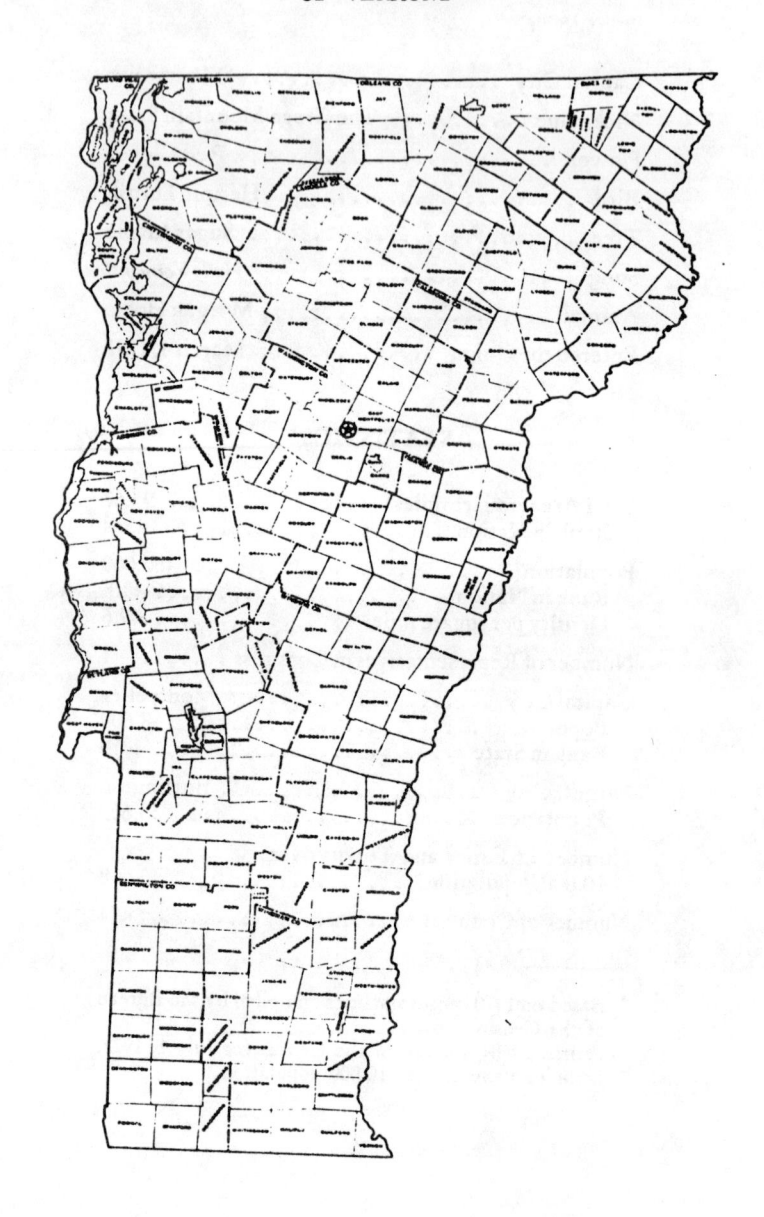

SELECTED BIBLIOGRAPHY

Allen, Ira. *The Natural and Political History of the State of Vermont.* London: Printed by J. W. Myers, 1798.

Carpenter, William Henry and Arthur, T. S. *The History of Vermont from Its Earliest Settlement to the Present Time.* Philadelphia: Lippincott, Grambo and Company, 1853.

Collins, Edward Day. *A History of Vermont.* Boston: Ginn and Company, 1916, rev. ed.

Conant, Edward. *The Geographical History, Constitution and Civil Government of Vermont.* Rutland, Vt.: The Tuttle Co., 1907.

Crockett, Walter Hill. *Vermont, The Green Mountain State....* New York: The Century History Company, Inc., 1921. 4 vols.

Folsom, William R. *Vermonters in Battle and Other Papers.* Montpelier: Vermont Historical Society, 1953.

Hall, Benjamin Homer. *History of Eastern Vermont, from Its Earliest Settlement to the Close of the Eighteenth Century.* Albany: J. Munsell, 1865, 2 vols.

Hall, Hilard. *The History of Vermont, from Its Discovery to Its Admission into the Union in 1791.* Albany, N. Y.: J. Munsell, 1868.

Hill, Ralph Nading. *Contrary Country, A Chronicle of Vermont.* New York: Rinehart, 1956.

Lee, John P. *Uncommon Vermont.* Rutland, Vt.: The Tuttle Company, 1926.

Ludlum, David McWilliams. *Social Ferment in Vermont, 1791-1850.* New York: Columbia University Press, 1939.

Newton, Earle Williams. *The Vermont Story: A History of the People of the Green Mountain State, 1749-1949.* Montpelier: Vermont Historical Society, 1949.

Thompson, Charles Miner. *Essays in the Social and Economic History of Vermont.* Boston: Houghton Mifflin Company, 1943.

Williamsum, Chilton. *Vermont in Quandary: 1763-1825.*

Montpelier: Vermont Historical Society, 1949.

NAME INDEX

Abbot, Stephen, 7
Addison, Joseph, 4
Aiken, George D., 14
Allen, Ethan, 2
Arnold, Benedict, 2
Arthur, Chester A., 7, 10
Arthur, Harold J., 14, 15

Baker, Remember, 2
Barstow, Joel L., 10
Bell, Charles J., 11
Billings, Franklin S., 13
Brigham, Paul, 5
Burgoyne, John, 2
Butler, Ezra, 7

Champlain, Samuel de, 1, 7
Chittenden, Thomas, 3, 4, 6
Clement, Percival W., 12
Collamer, Jacob, 8
Converse, Julius, 10
Coolidge, Calvin, 10, 13
Coolidge, Carlos, 8
Crafts, Samuel C., 7

Danning, Lewis, 7
Davenport, Thomas, 7
Davis, Deane C., 16
Dillingham, Paul, 9
Dillingham, William P., 11
Dole, Robert J., 17

Essex, Robert Devereux, Earl of, 5

Fairbanks, Erastus, 8, 9
Fairbanks, Horace, 10
Fall, Albert B., 13
Farnham, Roswell, 10
Fletcher, Allen M., 12
Fletcher, Ryland, 8
Ford, Gerald R., 16

Franklin, Benjamin, 5
Fuller, Levi K., 11

Galusha, Jonas, 6
Garrison, William Lloyd, 7
Garfield, James Abram, 10
Gates, Charles W., 12
George II, King of England, 10
Gibson, Ernest W., 14, 15
Graham, Horace F., 12
Grout, Josiah, 11

Hale, Ewel, 5
Hall, Hiland, 8
Harding, Warren G., 13
Harrison, Benjamin, 11
Hartness, James, 12
Hawthorne, Nathaniel, 9
Hendee, George W., 10
Hoff, Philip H., 15
Holbrook, Frederick, 9

Jennison, Silas H., 7
Johnson, Lyndon B., 15

Keyser, Frank Ray, Jr., 15

Laval, Bishop de, 1

Matlocks, John, 8
McCullough, John G., 11
Mead, John A., 12
Montgomery, General, 2
Morrill, Justin, 9

Nixon, Richard M., 16
Noyes, John Humphrey, 7

Ormsbee, Ebenezer J., 11

Page, Carroll S., 11
Page, John B., 9
Paine, Charles, 8
Palmer, William A., 7
Peck, Asahel, 10

Pingree, Samuel E., 11
Proctor, Fletcher D., 12
Proctor, Mortimer Robinson, 5
Proctor, Redfield, 10, 11
Prouty, George H., 12

Robinson, John S., 8
Robinson, Joseph R., 15
Robinson, Moses, 4
Royce, Stephen, 8

Salmon, Thomas P., 16
Sargent, John G., 13
Schulyer, General, 2
Skinner, Richard, 6
Smith, Charles M., 14
Smith, Edward C., 19
Smith, Israel, 6
Smith, John Gregory, 9
Snelling, Richard, 17
Solzhenitsyn, Alexander I., 17
Stafford, Robert T., 15
Stark, John, 2
Stewart, John W., 10
Stinckney, William W., 11

Tichenor, Isaac, 5, 6

Van Ness, Cornelius P., 7

Warm, Jacobus de, 1
Wagner, Seth, 2
Washburn, Peter T., 9, 10
Washington, George, 3, 6
Weeks, John E., 13
Wentworth, Benning, 3
Wentworth, John, 1
William IV, Prince of Orange, 3
Williams, Carter K., 8
Wills, William Henry, 14
Wilson, Stanley C., 13

Woodbury, Urban A., 11

Yough, B. H., 9